MANIPULATED

MANIPULATED

THE 12 DEADLY LIES OF NETWORK MARKETING

MARK DAVENPORT

MANIPULATED
BOOKS

MANIPULATED

The 12 Deadly Lies of Network Marketing

ISBN   978-1-5445-0394-3 *Hardcover*

978-1-5445-0393-6 *Paperback*

978-1-5445-0392-9 *Ebook*

To my wife and parents

CONTENTS

INTRODUCTION

In the world of direct marketing, there are many ways to sell products and services to the public, but the two that have garnered the most controversy are multilevel marketing (MLM) and network marketing (NWM). Over the years, I have provided coaching, either directly or indirectly, to seventy-six different multilevel and network marketing companies, helping them with launch strategies, educational concepts for their distributors, developing standard operating procedures (SOP), coordinating leadership development and communication strategies, and helping them develop and integrate new technology, among many other things.

Looking back at all of the companies I've worked with, I would say that only six of them were good, solid companies able to live up to their promises and survive long term in the market. A couple of them, which I assumed would last, disappeared literally overnight. In examining the downfall of so many, I've found that too many of them relied on deception and phony promises. They seemed like great companies selling what appeared to be great products, but they were all built on hype.

In many cases, the founders of these companies had success in other industries, so they assumed they would achieve success with the network marketing formula. After all, the salespeople and owners of big, successful network marketing companies all claim this model is super simple and easy to implement. In reality, the opposite is true.

Even companies with billion-dollar holding companies backing them have run into major problems and shut down. They didn't anticipate the relentless negative press or hate directed at the industry. When they finally realized just how harsh it was, some of them said, "This isn't worth the risk to our reputation or potential legal trouble."

THE HARD WAY

Everything I've learned about multilevel marketing, I've learned the hard way. My father was a professor, and all my siblings are intellectuals. Going to university was expected, so that's what I did. I studied philosophy and economics and earned a sports diploma, and I had no intention of becoming a businessman.

Then one day, I received a call because a friend had recommended me to a company that sold insurance. "Your friend thinks you're crazy determined to make money," the salesperson said. He pitched me a multilevel marketing program with an opportunity to get paid based on performance instead of education. It sounded like a good deal—a fast track to success.

I accepted the offer and signed up. The company's main purpose was selling to customers. Once you became good at selling, you earned the right to train people who would recruit others into your business; but I quickly ran into a problem. As a college student with little sales experience,

I was so nervous on the phone I could barely say my own name.

The guy who recruited me had promised, "I will be on your side, so if you have any questions, contact me. We will do this together." Since I was struggling with my sales calls, I reached out to him and other people up through the ranks.

"You guys promised you would help me," I said. "I really need training on how to complete a sales call properly. I have the script, and I know I'm supposed to read it, but it doesn't work for me. I've pitched to a hundred people, and every single one of them said no."

They all brushed me off. I heard many versions of, "I'm super busy right now, but I'll get back to you." During my time at that company, every single time I asked for help, I was told people had other appointments or would get back to me eventually or were just too busy. No one ever helped me with my sales calls.

It was the opposite of what they'd promised. I'd taken a semester off college to build this new career, and nobody would help or answer my questions. Even when I started having a little success, I still found that everyone upline had no time for me.

The problem had to do with the system itself. The higher

you climbed in the organization, the more money you made but the less money the person upline made from you. In other words, it was not to their advantage to help me close the gap, because it reduced their residual income from my sales.

When I realized this, I became determined. There are two responses to this kind of betrayal: either giving up or working harder. I decided to work harder. Though I knew I'd been lied to, I also knew I was responsible for my own success. Pointing fingers wasn't going to get me anywhere.

I worked harder than ever, and after a year, I finally figured out the sales model and began making real money. After the second year, I became one of the top sales leaders in the company. Even then, I continued to encounter lies and broken promises in the way the company was run. Eventually, I decided I'd had enough, so I left.

Afterward, I became a sales director for two other companies, and while I made money, I discovered again and again that leaders often preach one thing and do the opposite. Finally, I'd had enough. Taking the positive skills and habits I'd learned, I decided to start my own business.

I can certainly do better than being constantly lied to, I thought. I knew if I recruited just 10 percent of the good, hardworking, teachable people who had quit that first business because they were lied to, I could create the number one company in Germany—possibly Europe, maybe even the whole *world*.

So that's what I did.

A FAILURE OF DUE DILIGENCE

I started my own multilevel marketing company, recruited some of the great people who had left the previous company, and we went from nothing to $52 million in sales in twelve months. It seemed like things were going very well, but then I learned another lesson—always triple-check your business partners.

My business partner, whom I met through my network of professional contacts, was a nice guy who'd already made a lot of money. He drove expensive cars and had a lovely family. What I didn't know is that he'd been convicted for fraud earlier in his career. When our company started growing fast, our competition started to get annoyed. The district attorney was pointed in our direction, saw who my business partner was, and decided to open an investigation.

As it turns out, despite the fact that Germany is supposedly a democracy, the government can completely shut down your company while you're under investigation. That's exactly what they did. Two years later, I went to court and won the case; but by then, I'd already lost a ton of money.

Sadly, a week before the company was shut down, we'd won an award as the number one employer in our state. The mayor who had presented us with the award had an office in the same building, so he was there when the district attorney raided us. It was like a movie. Helicopters circled overhead, fifteen cars pulled up in front of the building. Government officials raided our office, my home, the bank we used, and the tech offices that worked with us. It looked like they were hunting down a team of mass murderers, but they were only looking for possible fraud from my business partner.

I lost the company overnight, and with it, almost $10 million in assets. It was a terrible time in my life. My wife, however, was a ray of sunshine through it all. The day of the raid, I came home and said, "Hey, darling, do you like our house and our nice cars?"

"Yeah," she replied.

"Well, we lost all of them today," I told her, "and I have no idea if we'll ever get them back."

Her only comment was, "Okay, well, that's how it goes sometimes. By the way, are you hungry? I made noodles for dinner."

That's when I knew I'd married the right woman.

LEARNING FROM AN AWFUL EXPERIENCE

After that awful experience, I could have played the victim, but I chose to learn from it. I would do my due diligence with any business partner, without fail.

Even though I won the case, I was hurt, and I lost confidence in my government, in their fairness and efficiency when it comes to investigations. In a sense, I felt like I'd lost part of my identity, so I decided to leave the country that I no longer felt connected to. Disgusted by my treatment, I emigrated from Germany, vowing never to return—and I haven't.

I went on to build another company and expanded it to nineteen different countries with half a billion USD in sales. Of course, when you work in nineteen countries, you learn that every country has its own laws, and no government trusts multilevel marketing, so you need an army of lawyers. At one point, I was spending as much as $400,000 a month on attorney fees.

I had all kinds of weird experiences during that time. The moment you create success, your competitors start working to get rid of you. I've had guns pulled on me during a meeting in a hotel lobby. Sued multiple times. Gone to court in eleven different countries—and won every single case. The amount of stress and the money and time consumed were crazy.

In all these experiences, I saw the same things happening over and over again. The same lies, dishonesty, and broken promises were being made in companies throughout this industry and around the world, and nobody seemed to be trying to fix the problem.

I decided to start implementing the change in my own company. So many multilevel marketing companies promise coaching and then don't follow through, or else they charge exorbitant fees for the coaching. I decided to offer no-cost coaching to every salesperson I brought on board. After all, it's good coaching that helps a gifted athlete achieve their true potential, and that's true of salespeople as well. I began teaching people to deal honestly, to avoid the lies and exaggerations that are so common, and to tell the truth about our products and services.

This coaching was so successful that I sold my company at the age of forty, became semi-retired, and started offering these strategies to other companies. I've seen this honest, straightforward approach make such a difference in so many companies, it's clear I'm onto something.

AN HONEST LOOK

Everyone knows the industry is full of dishonest claims and outright lies, but there seems to be a nonverbal agreement in which company leaders and salespeople say, "If I stick my neck out to talk about it, I'll be the first one to go down. I'd better go with the flow."

Seeing this attitude in company after company over the course of twenty years, I finally decided it was time to take an honest look at the industry. With so few books written that deal with this specific problem, I wanted to offer this resource, which stems from thorough research, to look closely at what's really going on. Some experts suggest that as many as 400,000 people enroll in a multilevel or network marketing business every month, so the problems endemic to this industry affect a huge number of people.

If this industry would stick to the facts—good or bad—and allow people to come to an educated decision, the entire industry would benefit. We would avoid most of the bad press that drives many of these companies out of existence, along with the threat of government regulations that could shut everyone down for good.

I have no interest in being a Monday-morning quarterback. I'm taking the message to the entire industry, warning people against making some of the stupid mistakes that I and others have made and showing them a better way.

MULTILEVEL MARKETING VS. NETWORK MARKETING

No matter what country you're in, if you approach a hundred people and ask them if they want to join your organization and become salespeople, the overwhelming majority will say, "Hell, no! I went to school to get a real job." In every country I've ever visited, salespeople are about as low on the social ladder as you can get. It's ironic because, without salespeople, no product or service would move. Yet, that's how it is. The deceptive practices often used by salespeople have created a negative reputation all over the world, and it's a huge problem in the multilevel marketing industry.

Let's clarify the key differences between multilevel marketing (MLM) and network marketing (NWM). They are both forms of direct marketing and the terms are sometimes used interchangeably, but they aren't quite the same thing. Multilevel marketing is about recruiting people to become good salespeople and, once they succeed, training them to expand the business by recruiting other salespeople. They are paid for their own sales, but they also get a percentage of the sales made by the team members they've recruited.

In network marketing, people first become customers and then they are encouraged to become *distributors* of the product. While a salesperson in an MLM company will ask customers for referrals in order to make more sales, in network marketing, the message goes like this: "Hey, try this product. You'll like it. If you like it, why don't you sign up to become part of my consumer-based team. Then you can buy the product at a reduced price, sell it to others, *and* make money for referrals."

To most people, that sounds a lot nicer than the MLM pitch, "Do you want to become a salesperson?"

Unfortunately, the pitch usually builds to some blatant lies: "You'll make passive income, and before you know it, you'll be living the high life and you'll never have to work again."

Network marketing has resulted in some well-known instances of government crackdowns, such as the Federal Trade Commission (FTC) leveling a $200 million penalty against Herbalife. In their ruling, the FTC forced Herbalife to restructure their business so that most of their income comes from sales to end consumers rather than incentivizing distributors to buy their products.

YOU'RE NOT ALONE

Instead of waiting for the FTC or other government regulatory bodies to step in and force change with massive penalties, we should deal with the problem ourselves. By discussing common industry lies, I hope to inspire decision makers to sit down together and seek ways to make changes at an industry level—to build long-lasting businesses without these negative tactics.

The lies I share in this book are so common, you will no doubt have encountered most of them in a sales pitch at some point in your life. No matter the country, no matter the culture, no matter the product that's being sold, the same lies are told everywhere. We can do better. As an industry, we *should* do better.

If you've been tricked, hurt, or ruined by any of the lies you read about in these pages, know that you're not alone. Many of us have fallen for them. We're only human, after all. Know that you can protect yourself.

In Part One, we will address the lies that companies tell about themselves—the ways in which they paint false pictures about their industry, founders, or products. In Part Two, we will examine the lies companies and leaders tell about the potential future success people will have when they join.

With the knowledge you gain here, the next time you're in a meeting somewhere and you hear one of these lies, you'll know how to unmask and counter it. If a company encourages you to use one of these lies, you will know not to get sucked in. More than that, you'll know how to build a culture based on integrity and truth that leads to a better business.

MEN ARE MORE SUSCEPTIBLE

Men are often far more susceptible to the wild promises and unsubstantiated claims of network marketing. Even though most of the industry is comprised of women, overwhelmingly, the men that I meet in network marketing are the ones perpetuating the lies we will discuss in this book.

Part of the problem is that these men are always looking for the next best opportunity. They buy into a company, work hard, start to achieve a bit of success, and then they say, "I made this happen. I'm so awesome, I deserve to get paid more." By that point, they might be earning six figures a year, which is fantastic, but it makes them want to strive for even more. That makes them susceptible to buying into the hype all over again—at another company. I've met so many men in this industry who worked hard, achieved success, then threw it all away on the next opportunity that came along.

Women account for 70 percent of industry leaders, but far more of them have realistic expectations about their possible success in network marketing, which shields them from the lies. Most women are in network marketing to help their loved ones or to supplement their income. They are satisfied making an extra $500 a month, and they don't get frustrated as easily when they fail to achieve a sales goal. Rarely are they the ones filling their garages with fancy cars, jumping from airplanes in their promotional videos, and pounding their chests while making ludicrous claims.

It's not clear whether this behavior is learned or innate, but I can't discount it. It seems to cross all national boundaries. Many of the men I meet have changed companies five, ten, or fifteen times. Sooner or later, most of them come to ruin. They are obsessed with the idea of owning a mansion, a yacht, or a private jet, and they are convinced it's going to happen. They embrace the hype, buy into the exaggeration, and go crazy for the latest gimmick.

Along the way, they promote those same lies, which degrades their credibility. When every company you've worked for is the most amazing thing since sliced bread, but you've worked for fifteen companies, eventually no one believes you. These guys drive away their whole network and reach a dead end in their careers.

These are the ones who need this book. They're the ones who can change the industry.

Know that what I share in this book is valuable information for men and women alike. I'm not judging or condemning anyone. I've been there. I've experienced the damage possible when you don't do your due diligence, when you buy into false promises and race ahead blindly because you want wild success.

Now it's time to break the cycle of lies. We can change the industry for the better. All of us working together can transform our reputation, reduce attrition, and create a healthier form of long-term success.

PART ONE

LIES ABOUT THE BUSINESS

LIE
ONE

NETWORK MARKETING IS LIKE GETTING PAID TO RECOMMEND A MOVIE

This is a lie I've heard in every MLM or network market-ing company I've ever encountered. It usually unfolds like this:

"Have you ever been to a movie?" the salesperson asks.

"Yeah, sure," the prospect replies.

"And you talked about the movie with your friends after-ward, didn't you?"

"Absolutely."

"You told five people, and then they probably told five

other people. Isn't that interesting? That's twenty-five people who heard about the movie. Then those twenty-five people probably told five people, which is 125. By the fourth level, 625 people have heard about and possibly bought a ticket to that movie, all because you talked to your friends about it. That's networking! Now imagine you got paid a little for each ticket someone in your network bought—that's networking marketing. Doesn't that sound good?"

The prospect might shrug and reply, "Yeah, I guess so."

"Great," the salesperson says, extending his hand for a hearty handshake. "Welcome to the team. If you can recommend a movie to your friends, you can succeed in this business."

Of course, in reality, networking marketing bears *no resemblance* to the scenario the salesperson just shared. First, just because you tell five friends about a movie doesn't guarantee they will tell anyone else. They might not care enough to tell anyone, or they might be too lazy to bother. They might not even have five friends.

Trying to turn marketing into a mathematical model or matrix fails to take in the human factor. Even your friends who want to see the movie might not spread the news. Human beings are unpredictable.

Second, the distribution model of network marketing works very differently from recommending a movie. If you tell your friends about a movie, they know exactly where to go to watch it. However, if you tell your friend about a "power tea" called *Terra-X* that antioxidizes and promotes hair growth, your friend will have no idea where to get it or how much it costs.

Also, if recommending movies was like network marketing, you would start by purchasing ten tickets and keeping them in stock. Then, the next time (and probably last time) you were invited to a party, you would try to pester absolutely everyone at the party to buy one of those tickets from you.

"Hey, this is the best movie ever," you would say. "You have *no idea* how good it is. Oh my God, the action scenes are amazing! Seriously, you saw the movie trailer, and you think you know how good it is, but the trailer can't even do justice to this amazing movie. Just let me describe a few of the best scenes to you. Oh, and the dialogue is so awesome. I'll give you some of my favorite quotes. I was moved by the story. It made me think. It made me a better person. You'll be talking about it with your friends for *years*. If you had any idea how awesome this movie is, you'd buy a ticket right now while you still can. It's going to be a big deal. Everyone will be talking about it. Anyone who misses this movie will really feel left out. Don't you want to buy a ticket right now—I mean *right now?*"

Almost everyone at the party would say the same thing: "No!"

In the unlikely event you talked someone into it, you wouldn't even give them the ticket. Instead, you'd say, "You will love this movie so much, I want you to buy all ten tickets and go sell them to your friends over in the corner there."

Suddenly, it doesn't sound so easy.

Versions of this lie are told constantly. People share it onstage at big events because it's so relatable. It's also passed around in personal meetings, on webinars and during Zoom conferences. Anywhere recruitment takes place, this lie is told.

Jay Martin, founder of National Safety Associates, which used to sell air and water filters before switching to supplements, famously started every meeting with this lie. He loved to say, "Isn't it wonderful to be in an industry that is *just like recommending a movie to a friend?*"

The crowd always went wild.

THE LOWEST PRICE POSSIBLE

Another common lie about network marketing is that it's

not as *cost-intensive* as other businesses. "The savings are passed down to both the distributor and the customer. After all, there are no warehousing costs, and because you are doing all of the marketing, there are no marketing costs. The end consumer gets the *lowest price possible*."

In reality, network marketing companies tend to be product-driven, and products need to be shipped. This requires warehousing because it's often illegal to ship from a single warehouse in the United States or China or Germany to end consumers. Every country has its own regulations and laws, so products often must be warehoused in the countries they are shipped to before they reach consumers.

Additionally, even if network marketing companies don't pay for TV, magazine, or newspaper ads, they certainly fund social media campaigns, which means they're almost certainly paying top dollar to run these campaigns during peak seasons like summer break. They're also paying for incentives such as world travel for their reps, car programs giving out "free" cars, monthly or quarterly promotions to push sales, and events and conventions to entertain reps around the globe. All of this costs a lot of money.

I heard a version of this lie at a big event not so long ago. The CEO of Bon Ami had created a slideshow that guided people through the elaborate infrastructure of warehousing and trucking at a traditional business. Then he showed an animated wrecking ball smashing it all to pieces.

"We don't spend that money," he announced to the crowd. "It all goes into your pocket!"

Later, they had a guy walk through the crowd with a microphone, pretending to be a shareholder. He approached seemingly random people and asked them, "What are you most excited about with this opportunity?"

The people he spoke to were almost certainly preselected, and they gave predictable answers—more freedom, more money, more growth potential.

Finally, he approached a man in the crowd who said, "If that slideshow is correct, then I guess I'm fired, because I run fifteen warehouses for your company."

BIGGER THAN ALL OTHER INDUSTRIES COMBINED

A common claim in this industry says that network marketing is bigger than *all other industries combined*. I particularly hate this lie because it's so easy to disprove with a simple Google search.

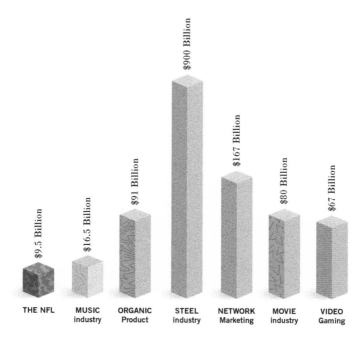

As you can see from the graphic, the steel industry alone is worth about $900 billion, while network marketing is worth a comparatively measly $160 billion. Despite this, a Google image search finds at least 1.6 million slides from presentations claiming that network marketing is the biggest industry by far. It's such a bold, blatant lie, it's crazy that people continue to use it.

I overheard a network marketing recruiter using this lie in his recruitment pitch.

"Network marketing is bigger than gaming and smart-phones," he told me.

While he spoke, I looked up the stats on my phone to show him how wrong he was, and he had no response. He seemed startled that the claim wasn't true.

To be fair, the first time I heard someone claim that network marketing is the biggest industry, I didn't search online for verification. It wasn't until the lie grew, until "the biggest industry" became "bigger than all other industries combined," that I felt compelled to seek proof. Within seconds of searching on Google, the lie was clear.

I can't comprehend how such intelligent, educated people, experts with MBAs and doctorates—intellectuals—can keep repeating this lie and *actually believe it*.

WHY DO THEY LIE?

For some reason, people in this industry feel compelled to overhype everything, even the things that are already good. It should be enough that the industry is huge and growing like crazy, but salespeople still think they have to make it sound even more attractive. I've heard these lies from big companies like Herbalife and the ACN Network, both of which net billions of dollars in sales every year. They are already undeniably successful, but they continue to overhype.

When every company tells the same lies constantly,

people begin to switch off their skepticism. They assume the lies must be true, and they start getting excited working at a *low-cost* industry that is *bigger than all other industries combined*. The prospect of being part of something so special becomes powerful. It's like promoting the first fully 4D movie! It's like nothing else you've ever experienced in your life.

Why hasn't someone put a stop to these lies? Because it's a difficult task. Going against the entire industry, including the big, successful companies, could alienate potential partners and fuel bad blood. It's so much easier to just go with the flow.

"After all, everyone else is doing it."

SPOTTING THE LIES

The easiest way to spot a lie is to ask for more specific information. For example, if a salesperson claims, "Our process is just like recommending a movie," ask them, "To how many people have you recommended your product?" At that point, they will almost certainly see an opportunity to brag and quote a big number.

"I've told a hundred people!"

At that point, all you have to do is ask, "How many of

those hundred bought from you and became part of your network?"

On the spot, the salesperson will most likely make up a number erring on the high side to look good.

"Twenty!"

You should be able to verify the existence of those twenty customers. Though distributors in this industry aren't good at tracking consumers, ask to see the back-office numbers. All network marketing companies use a back office to control the business, and the actual numbers aren't a secret. Without giving away any sensitive customer data, the salesperson should be able to back up their claim with a specific list of clients in their network.

You can also look up their claims online. Try a simple Google search, but be careful not to fall for the first response you see. People tell lies online as well as they do in person. Just because a claim tops the search results on Google doesn't make it true. Marketers buy traffic to specific keywords. If you search for a company's name followed by the word "scam," you shouldn't necessarily trust the information provided by the top result. It might be there because of a marketer buying traffic for the term "scam." Make sure you get information from trustworthy sources.

WHY DOES THE INDUSTRY HAVE SO MANY LIARS?

The network marketing industry doesn't specifically attract liars. Rather, it attracts three kinds of people: those seeking community, those who are fans of specific products, and those who are very ambitious.

Seeking Community

With the decline of churches as foundations of their respective communities, people often long for an alternative. Network marketing appears to offer a community where people think alike, feel alike, and all work together to achieve a dream. Sales alone doesn't bring fulfillment, but when people sit together at conferences, it seems to fill the emptiness.

Fans of the Product

Other people don't care so much about the community. They are such fans of specific products that they feel the need to share them. Typically, they've had a positive experience with a product, so they want others to have the same experience. Most of these people are genuinely good, decent individuals who care about others.

Ambitious

Finally, some just dream of living the rock-star lifestyle. They are driven by ambition and a desire for success. Unfortunately, of the three, this group is the most likely to spread these common industry lies. I compare them to athletes. As an athlete myself, I know the temptation to seek any little advantage—a little red pill, a better pair of shoes, some magic health drink. It's always hard for me to condemn athletes who get caught doping, because I know how frustrating it is when you're the only one fighting fair. It's easy to rationalize doping. "Everyone does it. That's just the way it is." I never cheated as an athlete, because I don't want the bad karma or troubled conscience, but I fully understand why people do it. Resisting the urge to cheat requires a strong moral compass and the ability to stay focused in the face of temptation.

In most cases, cheating only brings short-term success. Many athletes have enjoyed a few years of success due to cheating, only to eventually get caught and permanently destroy their reputation. In the same way, if a salesperson tells his friends these common lies about network marketing and his friends decide to Google his claims, his reputation will take a hit.

I hope that by reading this book, some people in the industry will do their due diligence, learn to spot the lies, and avoid them at all costs. That's the path to long-term success.

If a company claims they've cut out the middleman and reduced costs, begin by researching the company's website for an overview of how the business operates. Then look up any offices or warehouses they use to see if the reality matches the claim. This can usually be done online.

The same goes for recruitment campaigns. Recruiters often brag about their constant promotions. "We always have summer campaigns. If you work for us, you'll have plenty of help." This can all be verified online.

HONEST WAYS TO DESCRIBE NETWORK MARKETING

None of these lies are necessary. On the contrary, network marketing companies can achieve tremendous success while *constantly telling the truth.*

If you're an industry leader, recruiter, or distributor, break the trend! If you tell the truth, you become invincible. Nobody will ever complain that they were tricked into the business. Telling the truth shifts the burden of responsibility for success from the salesperson to the distributor. If you tell the truth and a friend joins the business, you still have a commitment to them, but they aren't entering under false pretenses. They know what they are getting into and what it will require to succeed.

This business can work, but rarely does it work like recommending a movie. Even when it does, that approach is only effective for "fans" of the product. Fans will naturally talk about a product they're passionate about. They don't approach it like a business; the passion is sincere.

"You look great," someone might say. "Have you lost weight?"

"Yes, I have," they will respond. "I'm using this great diet pill. I love it."

"Can I try it?"

"Yes, you can. I will get you the contact information of the guy I'm buying it from."

It's an honest appreciation of the product that generates interest authentically.

For most people, however, that is not the situation. You have to avoid presenting two different stories about how your company works: one that is the truth and another that is the sales pitch.

When you make a pitch for how your process works, use an example that describes the real experience of working in this industry.

I like to compare it to a *franchise*:

"In 2016, the average investment in a franchise was $125,000," I will say. "On the other hand, the average investment in network marketing is between $49 and $299. As you can see, network marketing is much cheaper than buying a franchise, but it includes many of the same advantages. For example, distributors receive the product and all of its materials. They don't need to develop or invent anything. You sell the product using a strategy that the company has designed, tested, and proved—a strategy that doesn't use any lies. The work is similar to running a franchise—distributors recruit business partners and exercise leadership."

In all of this, I stick to the facts. I tell them that network marketing is a $160 billion industry, which is impressive considering that the industry has only been around for about forty-five years.

"It may not be the biggest industry," I admit, "but it has seen some of the biggest growth numbers of the last ten years."

The truth offers plenty of *facts* to get a potential partner excited.

A PERSONALIZED APPROACH

Honestly, when I was first pitched on network marketing, what got me excited was the honest, personalized approach of the salesperson. He started by saying, "I heard you're a determined athlete who never quits a job before it's finished."

"Yeah, that's true," I replied.

"I also heard you have big dreams for your life."

"That's true as well," I said.

Clearly, he had spoken to my friends and learned important details about my life, which allowed him to give a pitch that was highly personalized. This made it far more effective.

Before you pitch, think hard about the individuals you want to approach. Every pitch should be tailored to the listener, and always be clear about the qualities they bring to the table.

THE ONLY ONE FIGHTING FAIR

At first, you may feel like being honest puts you at a disadvantage, since all of your competitors are lying. Let's just admit it—dishonest pitches usually sound more appealing. However, you can turn the situation to your advantage.

Use your honesty as a selling point:

"The good thing about working with me is I believe in keeping it real. I'm always honest. I won't try to get you to join the company under false pretenses or by using phony promises. What you see is what you get. If you have any doubts about any of my claims, do your homework. I'm not trying to strong-arm you or trick you into signing away your life today. I want you to have a *crystal-clear* understanding of how this business works, so you can decide if you want to commit."

With a pitch like that, you put the choice and responsibility in your potential partner's hands. If he buys in, he will never come back to complain about some unrealized, impossible promise.

"Hey, you told me I would make $20,000 a month!"

Instead, he is setting his own goals.

Keeping it real is the *secret sauce* that keeps you *safe*.

THE FACTS ARE GOOD ENOUGH

Network marketing has created more income millionaires than any other industry, but it's not a handout. Anyone who wants to make money in this industry must be teachable. If someone thinks they already know everything they need to know to succeed at network marketing because they already enjoyed success in some other industry, network marketing might not be right for them. If anyone thinks they can achieve success at this without putting in a lot of time, they should move on.

It's like marriage. If I tell my wife that I'll never forget an anniversary date and then don't follow through, odds are a divorce is just around the corner. In the end, I lose 50 percent of my wealth. However, if I tell her, "I just don't care about anniversaries," and she still wants to marry me, then we're on a better track. She knows what she's getting into, so she's free to make an honest commitment based on facts.

Tell potential partners the truth:

"You have a real chance at success if you are teachable and willing to work. Entrance costs are lower than almost any other opportunity. At good companies, support systems are in place, so if you take your best shot, you can do well."

PRODUCT LIES

The lies in this chapter are only the beginning. In the next stage, we will learn about companies waxing poetic about the quality of their products. Often, product pitches include exaggerated stories, like the following:

"Let me tell you about the man stranded on an island who found an herb that miraculously cures a range of conditions."

Let's confront these product lies and work our way to a better truth.

LIE
TWO

OUR PRODUCT IS BACKED BY SCIENCE

When trying to motivate a potential partner, it's not uncommon to lie about a company's product, and one of the most common lies in this industry is the claim that a product is *backed by science.*

Xango is a company that sells a healthy juice drink. At every event, company leaders cruise the room bragging that their product is the only one in its class because of its FDA approval, but the FDA only reviews ingredients to ensure they're safe for the end user.

Any claim of FDA approval is false. The people who spread these claims usually can't keep the details straight. They hear the claim from their company and repeat it over and over, eventually adding new twists that take it even farther.

There are a few related lies I see across all the niches of the industry, whether the company is selling supplements or telecommunications equipment. One of the most common is the phrase "patent pending."

The company World Global Network used to produce and sell a health watch, the Helo, in a futile attempt to compete with smartwatches from giants like Apple and Samsung. Their pitch, in essence, was, "This watch can do all of the same core functions as an expensive smart-watch, but it also has a *patent-pending* feature that warns the wearer when they're about to get sick."

Naturally, they couldn't disclose exactly how the watch accomplished this, as they needed to protect their intellectual property. The truth is, "patent pending" is a lie companies use to create hype out of absolutely nothing. If a product doesn't seem competitive enough, this phrase adds a little mystery, and the partners love it.

IT'S UNIQUE!

Another common lie is the claim of *uniqueness*.

"Nobody is using this ingredient. We have no competition. No one else can sell it because we have exclusive rights."

This is a lie that might have been closer to the truth in the past. Today, there is no ingredient or technology on the planet that is truly unique to just one company.

Blackberry used to own 90 percent of all business phones. Now, they're barely worth mentioning. Then Apple thought they were unbeatable, but Samsung developed their own product based on their observations of the iPhone. Now, Samsung is on top of the sales charts.

It's fairly easy to copy a product, whether the product is a piece of technology, a supplement, or a delicious fruit drink. A competing company only has to bring the product to a professional lab and have it analyzed, reverse engineering their own version. This happens all the time, even with patented products. Sometimes, massive lawsuits ensue that result in years of arguing in court, while the reverse-engineered products continue to be sold.

No product is unique.

In most cases, a product exists because a third-class inventor copied someone else. If every product pitched by network marketing companies was developed by prestigious inventors using quality ingredients, companies wouldn't hesitate to tell the real story. They wouldn't need to lie.

THE MOST OVERHYPED PRODUCT I'VE EVER SEEN

The most overhyped product I've ever seen was a magic laundry ball. I first encountered it because a friend of a friend said it was the best thing since sliced bread. When I finally saw it, I realized it was little more than a plastic ball with a hole in it, but the company claimed that if you put it in the washing machine, it would clean your clothes with less energy and almost no soap. They had no scientific research or data to back up this claim, and no explanation as to how it was even possible. However, they did claim it was "patent pending" and invented by some mysterious scientists. None of their claims held up to even a little bit of internet research. They invented everything out of thin air.

Despite this, the scam netted around $600 million. That's a lot of money from selling plastic balls that did absolutely nothing. All they had to do was convince distributors to buy it.

The scam only stopped when the Federal Trade Commission stepped in and debunked all the claims, killing the product and shattering the company.

HOW TO SPOT PRODUCT LIES

Companies want potential distributors to believe that their product is the ultimate choice, a guaranteed success with no alternatives on the market. Sometimes products actually do have a few select ingredients that are expensive and hard to obtain, which means they have real stories they could tell.

Nevertheless, companies are tempted to embellish those stories and make exaggerated claims. Even if the company doesn't lie, it's almost impossible to keep all the distributors from introducing their own wild claims as they attempt to recruit partners. Without proper training to warn them which words and phrases to avoid, it's too easy to introduce dishonest phrases like "the only one" and "patent pending." In the short term, these phrases work, helping them to recruit and motivate faster, but in the long run, they are doing tremendous damage to the reputation of an entire industry.

Thanks to technology, spotting lies is easier than ever. In my younger days, if I'd heard someone claim, "Our product is the only one with ginseng extract FTP-212," I would have had to drive around to local libraries, reading books on alternative medicine to see if the claim was true.

These days, all I need to do is take my phone out of my pocket, open the browser, and type "Find product with ginseng FTP-212." Almost every time, relevant websites will pop up. It's so easy to do, but for some reason, many people fail to do it.

Even if a product passes the Google test, there might still be lies associated with the company's claim. To dig a little deeper, you can look at the company's white papers, in which doctors or scientists go into detail about how the product works. Most companies have white papers in order to establish credibility, but few potential recruits ask to see them. If a company can produce white papers, that doesn't automatically guarantee that every claim is true. The papers need to be read and verified by someone who understands the topic. Bringing in an expert can verify the claim.

If a company claims a patent is pending, ask for a copy of the registration number. The number can then be used to look up the application on the United States Patent and Trademark Office website, free of charge.

Doing a bit of due diligence doesn't make you a party pooper. Instead, it gives you a much better chance of building a strong, long-lasting business.

A BETTER WAY TO PROMOTE PRODUCTS WITH SCIENCE

If you're currently working for a network marketing or MLM company, you need to verify your own pitch to avoid making false claims.

There's a saying in this industry: "Use your own story. If you don't have one, use someone else's story." If a close friend tells you a product story that he claims happened to him, he's probably telling the truth. You can trust him enough to use his story in your own product pitches, as long as you admit it's not your own experience.

Of course, it's important to develop your own experience with a product, so you can tell your own story. Fight the temptation to claim a product has done something for you that it clearly hasn't done.

For example, don't promote a weight loss product when you're currently gaining weight. That makes for a terrible testimonial. If you've only lost ten pounds, stick to the facts. "Hey, look at me. I started with the product, and I've already lost ten pounds. Why not try it out?"

Never promise a specific effect (e.g., "You will lose twenty-five pounds in three months"). I see too many salespeople give in to this temptation. Desperate to close the deal, they make specific guarantees that the product can't consistently deliver. Even if the product delivers a certain result for one person, that doesn't mean it will deliver the same result for everyone. For example, omega-3 fatty acid improves heart health for most people, but not for everyone.

Limit yourself to stories that have happened to you, your family, or close friends. If you can't guarantee a result, be open about that. Instead of making phony claims, use suggestions of what might be possible. If there's clear science behind the product, share it. If the ingredients are good, proudly proclaim it, but never guarantee a result that you can't universally provide.

Only promote products to people who have a use for them. For example, in the case of nitric oxide, it's especially useful for athletes. The effects will be more noticeable for athletes than for couch potatoes. Marathon runners know their bodies well, including their recovery time, so they will be ideal subjects to test out samples of the product and provide feedback. If they experience a positive effect, they will also have an easier time talking about it.

A good friend of mine introduced me to the last business I worked for (and still work for), but he didn't give me a sales pitch. He knew I was training hard, so he offered me a free sample of a product that was supposed to help with muscle pain. As it happened, I was experiencing an ache in my shoulder, so I tried the product. To my surprise, my shoulder pain went away almost immediately.

This made me incredibly interested in learning more about the product and sharing it with my fellow athletes to see if the result could be duplicated. My friend had found the most effective way to introduce me to the product without making an actual pitch. He didn't share phony claims, wild stories, or bogus science. He said, "This might help," and let me try it.

Instead of making promises you can't keep, the best approach is to say, "I can't tell you what the product will do for you, but I can tell you what it has done for my family and me." Then share those true stories, followed by a call to action to try it out. You're not making a guarantee, but you are suggesting that they might experience a positive result based on the true stories you've shared.

OTHER PRODUCT LIES

Many companies also make exaggerated claims about the high demand for their product. After all, if everyone wants the product, shouldn't you?

LIE
THREE

OUR PRODUCT IS IN HIGH DEMAND

Many of the lies in this chapter have a kernel of truth, but they appeal to wishful thinking. Potential partners want something so badly that they stop asking questions.

Distributors might say, "This product is in such high demand that you absolutely don't have to do anything. People will beg you to let them buy it." Whatever form the lie takes, the message is that the product sells itself.

Of course the truth is, *nothing sells itself* except goods that serve a vital need, like food, water, and lifesaving medicine. For every other product on the face of the earth, you have to create demand or at least remind people that a hidden demand is waiting to be revealed.

This lie mixes fact with fiction, which makes it more insidious than many of the lies we deal with in this book. For example, a company might attempt to connect their product to some genuine vital interest.

"Isn't there a growing need to get healthy? Of course there is, so, as you can see, demand for our supplement is huge. Demand is so big, the supplement sells itself."

This statement is partly true. In most countries today, there is indeed a growing need for people to get healthy, and that does create a vital interest. No matter how successful you are in life, if you're not in good health you won't be able to enjoy that success. This is common sense.

The lie comes from connecting that vital interest to a product. A desire to get healthy doesn't necessarily translate into demand for a particular supplement.

To add credibility, leaders tend to invent demand numbers, often posting them on social media. A global company might scour every market, looking for the most impressive statistic: "In South America, we've had a 925 percent increase in sales!"

In the United States, company leaders like to appeal to a product's popularity in Europe: "It's the latest and greatest thing in France!"

On the crazy end of the spectrum, companies make claims that anyone with an ounce of common sense should reject out of hand. "Eighty percent of Australians use our product!" A claim like that should set off alarm bells, because if it was true, the company would already be making billions in sales.

When checked against the company's balance sheet, these kinds of claims rarely add up.

EXTRAVAGANT CLAIMS WITHOUT OVERSIGHT

Vemma is a network marketing company that sells dietary supplements. In 2015, they were branded a pyramid scheme by the Federal Trade Commission. Jessica Rich, director of the FTC's Bureau of Consumer Protection, specifically criticized their "extravagant income claims."[1]

Vemma was routinely saying things such as, "Eighty percent of all people use our energy drink. Sales are off the charts! Thanks to insane demand, we are making a crazy amount of money."

They even invented numbers to back up any fact-checking so they could convince potential distributors that the

---

1   "Vemma Agrees to Ban on Pyramid Scheme Practices to Settle FTC Charges," Federal Trade Commission, December 15, 2016, https://www.ftc.gov/news-events/press-releases/2016/12/vemma-agrees-ban-pyramid-scheme-practices-settle-ftc-charges.

product practically sold itself. When this came out, the founder of Vemma, Benson Boreyko, took a lot of heat. Though the company eventually came back, it seems unlikely that they will ever fully recover.

The lack of oversight in this industry is sometimes shocking. Herbalife once introduced a green tea that they claimed would boost energy. I tried it during a long drive, and it worked. I went from struggling to stay awake to being wide-eyed and alert. The tea was fantastic—it was also illegal. The supplement in the drink caused heart attacks in a few of their customers.

I was actually sad to see the product removed from the market, because it worked so well. I mean, it never gave *me* a heart attack. Still, I wonder how a product with such risks made it to market in such a massive company without anyone expressing concern.

Herbalife had similar problems with a line of weight-loss supplements that were popular in the 1990s and early 2000s. They claimed the product would cause customers to shed up to ten kilograms in five to fifteen days, but at every Herbalife convention, the distributors promoting the product on stage were all significantly overweight. The claim just didn't hold up to scrutiny.

Exaggerated demand is so common, I've heard examples

of it in almost every company I've come across. Consider the National Safety Associates (NSA) pitch for their air and water filters.

An NSA leader often started by saying, "Don't you agree everybody needs to breathe?"

The listener couldn't help but answer, "Yes, of course."

"Wouldn't it be better if you could breathe healthy air?" the NSA leader continued. "That's something everyone wants. Wouldn't you agree?"

"Yes, I suppose so."

"That's right," the leader said, closing the deal. "Everyone wants healthy air, so you might as well sign up for our air filter subscription program."

Ironically, the company no longer makes air filters because demand was so low. They've moved on to supplements.

WHY THIS LIE IS SO COMMON

The lie of high demand is ultimately a mind game. Companies want you to think that it's easy to become wealthy and successful. They want to convince you that selling their product will be like working at a Genius Bar on the day Apple releases a new product—the customers will line up to hand you their hard-earned money.

Founders, corporate leaders, and distributors work together to maintain this lie, even though everyone involved knows it's a lie. There is an unsigned, nonverbal agreement that the facts will be exaggerated in order to hook people faster.

Company leaders do it, in large part, because they can get away with it. They figure exaggerating demand is a smart strategy. They spice it up with a few embellished facts, and before they know it, they've created a deadly mix.

Even if this lie begins innocently—a slight hyperbolizing of reality that fits within the boundaries of their ethical standards—it gradually transforms into a massive, out-of-control beast as distributors tell and retell it. However the lie starts, it always winds up saying the same thing: "It's easy for anyone pitching our product to become wealthy because the product sells itself."

UNMASKING THE DEMAND LIE

Unmasking this lie requires a business environment check, which is difficult to do on your own. I've learned from personal experience that anytime I hear a brand-new, unheard-of product is the newest and greatest thing, my first instinct is to *doubt my own knowledge.*

"Wow, if it's this popular, I should have heard of it," I think. "What's wrong with me that I've missed out on this amazing product?"

That's the mind game companies want to play with you.

"We're the best. You haven't heard of us? Something must be wrong with you. You'd better correct the situation by buying it."

To prevent this situation, you need a strong network of trusted friends. For example, when I heard an exaggerated pitch from a G4 internet provider, I texted my friends. "Have you heard of this company? They claim to provide the fastest internet speed ever."

All of my friends said, "No, I've never heard of this."

Sometimes, when I text my friends, they back up a company's claims.

"Yes, I've heard of that company. Their product is amazing."

Although this method doesn't provide empirical data, it

usually gives fairly accurate evidence of whether or not demand is high. If a company says everyone wants their product, shouldn't "everyone" include at least a few of your close friends?

Bear in mind, most people react badly to multilevel or network marketing. Studies in many countries indicate that network marketers have a lower status in society than bartenders or garbage collectors. Consequently, when you ask friends for advice, avoid leading with the phrase, "I'm thinking about getting involved in this network marketing opportunity." They will have an immediate negative reaction and might not give you an honest answer. Their first instinct will be to protect you from being sucked into a scam, even if the opportunity is a good one.

For a more rigorous approach, use Google Trends, a fantastic tool that shows which keywords are trending online. It even breaks the data down by location and time of day. I recommend using Google Trends to analyze the key phrase a company uses to generate buzz. Google has the largest collection of data on Earth, so if they can't find evidence of company demand, then demand simply doesn't exist.

If a company claims that products with omega-3 fatty acids are in high demand, you can check Google Trends and find out if they're telling the truth. A positive discovery can be rewarding. You now know for a fact that the demand is there, even if you have to channel it toward a specific product. Google Trends will even provide insight on where to sell it, because it lets you sort data by geography and demographics.

THE VIDEO PHONE DEMAND TEST

I was sitting in the lobby of a Sheraton hotel in London when a guy began to pitch me on a telecommunications company called American Communications Network (ACN). This might date me, but the product he was pitching was an early version of a videophone.

"In the olden days, people use to say, 'Wouldn't it be great if we could talk to someone far away,' and then they invented telephones," he said. "Suddenly, you could talk to someone far away. Now, people want to talk to people far away and *actually see them face to face*. We're on the forefront of this new frontier!"

This was years before FaceTime, so he was able to claim, "Everyone wants to be able to look at the person they're talking to on the phone. There's nothing better."

"I don't want to look at people while I'm talking on the phone," I replied, "and I'll bet I'm not alone on that."

I proposed a little test.

"We're in a packed lobby," I said. "Go over to that table of footballers, show them your product, and ask them if they want it."

The guy pulled out the product—it was quite ugly, massive, and clunky—and approached the table. To cut a long story short, he almost got beaten up by the footballers because they thought he was playing a practical joke. They assumed nobody would be selling such an ugly product that offered a service nobody wanted.

With one small test, I was able to see that the massive demand for this product didn't exist—at least, not in that specific form.

HOW TO AVOID USING THIS LIE

Stick to the facts, because they're often good enough to build excitement—and if they aren't, then you should consider changing companies. Avoid overhyping numbers. Just use what you already have.

The founders of your company are almost certainly invested in the product. They want it to succeed, so they've probably already done research. Companies don't choose products, industries, or markets that are destined to fail. That's why so many network marketing companies sell skincare products, supplements, and services such as electricity deals or telecommunications contracts. These are products that most people use, so there's a built-in demand, as evidenced by numerous billion-dollar companies in those industries.

Gather some real facts. Look at Google Trends. You might learn, for example, that there's a 1,600 percent increase in interest about omega-3's impact on heart health. That's a real fact you can use in your product pitch. Find credible sources that you can quote; avoid hearsay.

Theoretically, if you wanted to pitch FaceTime, you might say, "Many people use smartphones, but what if we added a function that allowed you to see your family *right now*. Would you agree that most people enjoy seeing family members who are far away?"

This is a reasonable pitch that appeals to the provable popularity of smartphones and the common-sense knowledge that people tend to love their own families.

If you want to include a claim based on market research, you need to find real numbers. Using our last example, you can truthfully claim, "Out of 325 million people, 240 million use smartphones—almost 75 percent.[2] That means we can approach 75 percent of people in the next twelve months about our FaceTime app."

If you stick to the facts and emphasize the importance of educating people about a product's advantages, you and your partners will be in a better position to go out and create demand.

IT'S ALWAYS THE PERFECT TIME

An exaggerated claim of demand for a product is almost always tied to a compelling lie about *perfect timing*. It's not enough that people want it; it also has to be the right time for you to sell it. That's the lie we'll examine next.

---

2   "Number of Smartphone Users in the United States from 2010 to 2022 (in Millions)," Statista, https://www.statista.com/statistics/201182/forecast-of-smartphone-users-in-the-us/.

LIE

FOUR

IT IS THE PERFECT TIME TO START WITH OUR COMPANY

Whether they've been on the market ten years or only a few months, every company claims it's the perfect time to start working with them. Clearly, this makes no sense. How can every point in a company's timeline be the perfect time?

Companies tend to portray themselves as fast-growing and consistently successful, but they often lack a reasonable explanation for the ups and downs in their history—ups and downs that happen in every market. In his book *The Dip*, Seth Godin explains that it's impossible to build a business without experiencing an occasional dip.

Still, many leaders and distributors in network marketing

don't want to face that fact. Compelled by wishful thinking, they prefer to believe that success will always come easily, and this attitude works its way into every pitch.

Brand-new companies tend to lengthen their timelines, trying to give the impression that they've been in the market for many years, just waiting for the right time to launch. This lie is an attempt to avoid the harsh reality that 80 percent of all startups, across the board, will fail in the first two years. This is true whether it's a brick-and-mortar, e-commerce, or franchise business.

If a company is still in that two-year window, they have to find some way to communicate a long history. "Our founders have been in business for twenty years. They spent the last eight years preparing the launch of this company, and we're finally ready to launch."

What they fail to mention is that the company is essentially an experiment, and potential partners are the guinea pigs.

ADVANTAGES AT EVERY MOMENT

Every point in a company's timeline has some advantages that could be truthfully leveraged in promoting the company. If you join a company in its early days, after a bit of due diligence, you have a better chance of making a lot of money as an early adopter. As long as the company has solid people and a great product, you will be well positioned to take advantage of early growth. New startups should promote that fact.

On the other hand, if a company has been in business for ten years or more, they're less likely to go out of business. They've had years to lay a solid foundation that can help the company weather hardships. Herbalife paid a $100 million penalty to the FTC and it didn't kill the company. They're still going strong. Every expert said they were finished, but all they had to do was increase sales in other markets.

It might be a little harder to pitch a product with the name Herbalife attached to it, but many of their products still make sense. The company is probably here to stay, so both distributors and customers can have a positive experience.

Entertainment Express was a Scandinavian company that, for some reason, sold DVDs in the internet era. Even when they were only a year old, they recruited people by claiming that their founders had spent eight years researching the market. They didn't last long. As it turned out, the founders had spent those eight years studying how to take a lot of people's money and run away with it.

Another network marketing company, Lyoness, is still around and still lying. They've invented their entire success story out of whole cloth. When they started, they merged with another company, but they never mention this in their sales pitch. Instead, they've concocted a big success story for their discount shopping system, presenting crazy statistics on the internet and in their presentations.

In reality, they've had to relocate from country to country numerous times in order to avoid prosecution. Their numbers are far from reality and their success story is a blatant lie.

LIES ABOUT GROWTH SPEED

The lies companies tell about their success often go hand in hand with lies about the *speed of their growth*.

"We expanded into fifteen countries within a year," they might claim, when the reality is, they've just opened branches in those countries after multiple shutdowns due to legal problems.

A new company, Devide, sells overpriced and overhyped watches and sunglasses by boasting about the valuation that the watches are bound to attain. The founder, Marcus Dahlgren, has claimed in podcasts that his watch brand will be sold within five years for $1 billion. There isn't a single reason to believe this will be the case.

Both growth numbers and time periods are often exaggerated. Even if a company's website says they've operated in a given country for ten years, you can look up the truth fairly easily. You might find that they only began marketing operations two years ago. This is meant to obscure the fact that the company has had a few crashes along the way. In doing so, they create an expectation of consistent business success that they can't possibly achieve.

AN OVERINFLATED COMPANY VISION

A lie that drives me crazy is *overinflated company vision*. I wonder sometimes if leaders from multiple companies don't meet together secretly and say, "Hey, let's see which of us can come up with the craziest company vision, because people seem to like that."

One company leader then says, "Our goal is to become the next billion-dollar company."

Another company leader counters, "Well, *our* company will become the first *trillion-dollar* company."

Then a third company leader boasts, "We're going to be

ten times bigger than Coca-Cola, Pepsi, and Morinda combined."

Consider QNet (aka QuestNet, aka GoldQuest), whose company leaders were boasting, with straight faces, that they would become bigger than Apple. On stage, their recruits would often say, "Name ten of the biggest companies on the planet, and we will beat all of them combined." Instead of laughing at the ludicrous claim, the crowd always clapped and cheered.

Vanilla was a company that sold American Eagle coins in Europe. Their vision was to take over the entire banking industry. It's hard to imagine a CEO being crazy enough to make such a claim, much less believe it. Imagine creating a small financial startup and making the entire global financial industry your enemy.

Why can't companies create a realistic company vision? These would still be impressive. I've seen plenty of great success stories in this industry, so why all the exaggeration?

WE'RE JUST LIKE GOOGLE

Another common lie is to *compare the company with Google or Microsoft*. It usually goes something like this: "Have you heard that the people who started at Google or Microsoft early took their bonuses in company shares? That's why there's a Millionaire Street in Seattle. It's where all of Microsoft's secretaries live in their million-dollar villas."

This spin is specifically designed to entice people to become early adopters. "This is your one-time shot to get in early on the next Microsoft!" It works well on people who only want to invest a small amount of time and money but still achieve amazing success.

Increasingly, these comparisons are shifting from Google and Microsoft to Uber and PayPal, but the purpose is the same.

Of course, these comparisons only work for very young companies. A company that has been around for years can't promise the advantages of early adoption. Instead, an older company will often say, "In the beginning, we had nothing—no support, no finances, nothing. Now, we've worked out all the problems and overcome all the obstacles. You are now entering *dreamland!* Just start selling these products, which are backed by science and *in massive demand*, and you will reap the rewards. That's the benefit of entering the game late."

There's a grain of truth in both of these claims. Yes, being an early adopter can be lucrative if the company hits big. Yes, there are fewer headaches getting involved in a company that has been around for a long time. This reality should be enough, but companies still exaggerate.

THE SECRET IS COMING

I often hear both new and old companies claim, "We have found the secret path to success, but *we can't share the details just yet*. However, when we finally reveal it, your mind will be *blown*. It's outstanding! There's so much more coming, so get involved now while you still can." This hits the same psychological trigger as the "patent pending" lie.

Claiming to have a big secret is a common tactic. It helps with retention, because people don't want to leave if they're convinced things are about to get a lot better. When a concert has multiple artists, they usually put the less popular, or less talented, performers on stage first so the audience will stick around. This is a similar idea. "Don't leave yet. Things are about to get amazing. Just wait and see."

An upcoming revelation eliminates personal responsibility for success. All the distributor has to do is wait around. If things are mediocre right now, just keep plugging away. Eventually, the big reveal will change the game!

Understandably, even disappointed distributors are

reluctant to miss a potential "biggest opportunity ever." After all, we've already missed out on Uber and PayPal because we listened to the so-called experts who urged caution.

We've missed out on so many magical opportunities, so we think, "This time, I can't get left behind. I have to join the company and stick around. The big reveal is coming!"

WHY THIS LIE IS USED

Companies want listeners to think, "This is the *only* company for me. This is *the one I've been waiting for*. Outstanding success is here (or just around the corner)."

In sales training, instructors often talk about the triggers that bring people to a decision point, and one of the most important triggers is *urgency*. If a salesperson can convince a potential customer that the decision has to be made *now or never*, the sale is almost guaranteed.

In the network marketing industry, they often say, "Opportunity knocks twice or thrice, but never more than that. If you've already missed one or two big opportunities to get rich, this might be your last chance!" It's not an outright lie, but it does play fast and loose with possibilities.

Personally, I just want companies to tell the truth. Tell

potential partners that your product might be something great, but don't make absolute guarantees. Make it clear that the end result is always down to each individual's time, effort, and teachability. Stop playing mind games using an appeal to *urgency*.

If a prospect is pitched by multiple companies, they usually go for the most exciting over-the-top one. We're only human. We think, "This opportunity is the one that will most impress my friends."

After all, which of the following pitches sounds more exciting?

- "It's a good product. It has been on the market for fifteen years. Though it contains ingredients you can find in many products, we've worked hard to get into multiple markets. I think it's a good opportunity for you."
- "We have a secret, patented product that everyone wants, and we're using a strategy that is so secret, I can't even talk about it. Since our company is in its early days, it's a great opportunity to buy in relatively cheaply and reap massive rewards down the road. Think about how rich you would be if you'd spent a thousand dollars on Bitcoin five years ago! You'd already own multiple mansions."

Based on emotion alone, most people would choose the

second pitch. The possibility that it might be true is just too exciting to pass up.

HOW TO SPOT THE LIES

As always, my favorite first step for spotting timeline lies is Google. Search for the date the company was founded. Their home page might not tell you, but business news sources should.

If a company claims to have been on the market for eight years and has a million customers spending $100 a month, that adds up to $1.2 billion a year, as much as $10 billion over the life of the company. This should be verifiable online.

Recruiters in this industry are bad at examining the connections between their claims, and the numbers rarely add up. They love tossing around impressive figures, and since most people don't attempt to verify, companies grow more confident about the spin over time.

Always take notes during meetings. During the pitch, do simple math to see if the numbers make sense. Don't be afraid to interrupt the recruiter or salesperson and say, "Why don't your numbers add up?" You will get some funny looks and mumbled denials, but you'll also unmask the lie.

THE TRUTH ABOUT PERFECT TIMING

The truth almost always comes out eventually. It's like dating. If you want to find an amazing spouse, you have to sell yourself by outlining your positive qualities. If you brag about your fantastic mansion and piles of money, while promising to cook, clean, and wait on them hand and foot, you might make a great impression. However, eventually, they're going to visit your home and see that you live in a filthy one-bedroom apartment, and your hopes of a relationship will be ruined.

There are plenty of great reasons to join both new and more established companies without resorting to lies. When building a long-term company, limit yourself to facts that can be verified.

A sales pitch based on the truth might sound something like this:

"Our company was founded nine years ago, and we've been able to achieve success by staying true to our mission. Our company is represented in thirty-six countries, and we've produced $50 million in sales. That number can be verified through documents released publicly by the company. We are stock-listed, and here's a website where you can check it out. Now is a good time to get started with us because we've laid the groundwork for stable growth in years to come."

This pitch sounds exciting enough without adding any embellishments, and the facts presented are verifiable. This is the kind of pitch people would feel comfortable committing to, and, better yet, they will avoid the heartache of learning you lied to them.

SUPERHUMAN CELEBRITIES

It's not uncommon for the founders of large companies to become mini-celebrities. Seeing the examples of Warren Buffett, Bill Gates, and Steve Jobs, many network marketing companies tell fabulous lies about their founders to sell them as almost superhuman in an attempt to make the company itself look better by association. That's the lie we'll look at next.

LIE
FIVE

OUR FOUNDER CREATED THIS COMPANY AFTER A LIFETIME OF SUCCESS

An oft-repeated lie, which appears in many variations, is the amazing tale of the incredible successes of a company's founder. These successes are said to have taught the founder everything they needed to know about how to create astoundingly successful businesses.

A recent example of this is Trump University, which paid $25 million in a fraud lawsuit in early 2018. The founder of the company, Donald Trump, claimed that the lessons taught in the university would guarantee the future success of students, all of whom paid between $500 and $25,000 to attend classes.[3]

---

3   Doug Criss, "A Judge Has Finalized a $25 Million Settlement for Students Who Claim They Were Defrauded by Trump University," CNN, April 10, 2018, https://edition.cnn.com/2018/04/10/politics/trump-university-settlement-finalized-trnd/index.html.

Not only did the basic premise prove false, but students didn't learn anything close to what was promised. Several lawsuits were filed, which were later combined into a class action suit, and there may be more penalties coming in the future. This provides a recent example of how founders can use some of their accomplishments, which might be true, to tell a story about a company that isn't true at all.

I experienced a similar lie firsthand at a meeting of the Global Consumer Group. I was invited to one of their meetings in 2010, during which their founder was introduced as a man who had started more than a hundred companies in his career. The claim kept growing, peaking at 170 companies.

When the founder took the stage, he explained his amazing new business idea: getting a large group of consumers to buy products in bulk in order to get lower prices. He hyped something called the "Founder's Package," which offered early entry buy-in with higher potential profits. It was an unimpressive idea that depended entirely on the founder's supposed success story, a claim driven home by the additional boast that he'd founded all of his companies by the age of forty-two.

When he asked if anyone in the room wanted a Founder's Package, I was the only person who didn't raise his hand. A few people even shouted, "We're going for it!"

Before long, everyone began staring at me, wondering why I was the one oddball who wouldn't raise his hand. Why would I dare miss out on such an exciting opportunity?

They got their answer pretty quickly.

Suddenly, police burst into the room, surrounded the founder, and slapped handcuffs on him. As we later learned, he had committed fraud at least fifty times already. The meeting was his last-ditch attempt to make some money before fleeing the country.

YOUR OWN PERSONAL JESUS

I get infuriated at the way companies try to sell their founders as holy men—your own personal Jesus—who don't care about making money. They've come along to make your life better, and that's all they care about. They want to:

- Make the world a better place.
- Give back the community.
- Make a difference in the lives of ordinary people.

Take your pick.

These lies place founders on a pedestal, so mere mortals

will cheer and shout, "What an honor to work with this wonderful person!"

To be fair, I have met a few founders who really are like that, but they are usually people who have already achieved millions in some other industry. Now, having more money than they could ever spend, they want to give other hopeful entrepreneurs the same opportunity.

Those kinds of founders are the exception. The vast majority are in it for the money.

Vanilla, the company that sold American Eagle gold coins, provides one of the saddest examples of an overhyped founder. The founder, Daniel Deubelbeiss, claimed he wanted to help people achieve financial independence, and his gold coins were meant to provide a base to invest in bigger businesses. At the time, cryptocurrencies didn't exist, so these were real gold coins.

To entice people, Vanilla spun a story about the founder that went something like this:

"Once upon a time, an investment banker saw how many billions were being made behind closed doors by big banks, so he decided to fight them. With his new company, he intends to conquer the banking industry and bring success to the masses."

Everyone who bought into the sales pitch thought of the founder as some kind of noble warrior-poet fighting to save the world. Sadly, when the company shut down, the founder took a huge amount of investor money and fled.

BETTER THAN ALL OF US

All of these founder lies are attempts to keep people from asking questions. Humans tend to be naturally skeptical, but if the founder is presented as moral, generous, and wealthy—a paragon of virtue—most people will feel too intimidated to question him.

When the founder seems so far above your grade, it's hard to raise your hand and say, "Can I please ask you a few questions about your success story? A few things don't add up." You run the risk of looking like a jerk at the meeting.

There have been so many fraudulent founders I can't list them all.

The worst I've ever encountered was the founder of a company called Nexagen. Their scam would be funny if it wasn't so sad. The founder, Roy Leyland, built a kind of cult. Instead of talking about products or money-making potential, his people felt compelled to follow the man.

"This guy is better than all of us," they said. "He makes

things happen. He has spent millions of dollars from his previous businesses to help disadvantaged kids and prevent addiction. He is literally saving the world."

Roy Leyland's story ticked all the right boxes to give the impression he had transcended the ordinary ways of life.

He preached the importance of a healthy lifestyle, and he always had a big plastic bottle of water on stage with him. A friend of mine invited me to attend one of his talks and give feedback. During the meeting, my friend got thirsty, and the only available water was Leyland's plastic bottle. My friend grabbed it and took a big sip.

It turned out to be straight vodka.

Rather than sipping healthy water on stage, the founder was gulping vodka by the liter. Suddenly, many things about Roy Leyland became clear.

Not long after this incident, bad news about the founder hit the news. Leyland had been caught using investor money to throw big parties and pay for drugs and prostitutes.

Roy Leyland was exactly the opposite of everything the company had professed him to be. Not long after, the company went broke, and Leyland disappeared. I don't know what ultimately happened to him, but since he was a gambling addict, I assume his story didn't end well.

More recently, we had the unfortunate example of Dr. Ruja Ignatova, founder of OneCoin, the latest company to jump on the cryptocurrency bandwagon. Cryptocurrency seems like the perfect MLM product: nothing to ship or send and almost no startup costs. Scammers *love* when there are no startup costs, because it's so much easier to "fake it until you make it."

Dr. Ruja Ignatova had been around for a while. She was a KPMG consultant to a number of top-fifty companies around the world. However, with OneCoin, she claimed she was ready to finally give to others a bit of the success she'd achieved.

OneCoin collected several billion dollars by selling people inventories of digital tokens. These tokens weren't even exchangeable cryptocurrency. The company claimed they would turn into cryptocurrency once the tech was in place.

Around January of 2018, news broke that Ignatova had disappeared. Nobody has seen or talked to her since (or, at least, nobody will admit to having done so). She's unavailable for meetings and communication. Many of her key leaders have moved on, and some of them have also disappeared.

Once again, the story of a successful founder wanting to make a difference in the world turned out to be a scam.

HOW TO SPOT FOUNDER LIES

As the saying goes, if something sounds too good to be true, it probably is. If the founder's story contains no mention of struggle or failure, it needs to be double-checked. An excellent resource is the Better Business Bureau website. In most countries, the BBB offers free access to all of its information.

Another option is to check the founder's credit ratings, though doing this is a bit trickier. However, in today's world, everyone and everything gets reviewed. Look for credible publications that have written about the founder in the past. If someone claims to have built many successful companies during the internet age, there will be stories online to verify the claim. No company enjoys secret success in the digital age.

Also, if a founder has a background in a specific industry, such as real estate or app development, you can look for that industry's "best of" lists, which can be found with a simple Google search. If the founder is truly the game-changer they claim to be, their achievements will be documented somewhere.

If you can't find evidence online, ask the founder or company leaders why that is. However, if you find evidence of multiple bankruptcies or fraud charges, run the other way.

I recommend the following internet search: "[Founder's Name] success story."

If a founder claims to have a charity, it should be easy to track down. Real charities are listed and registered, and they almost always have longstanding partners in the charity world. There should be a board of directors or some other oversight mechanism. Fake charities, especially those run by network marketing founders, will have a name and web page but no tax status, partners, or control mechanism.

As always, apply common sense. A person can't become a billionaire without becoming well-known.

Watch out for the old "World Trader" story about the founder who tripled or quadrupled their money through mysterious offshore stocks. I've traveled internationally and heard versions of this story everywhere. It's almost as common as the one about the mysterious relative who died and left the founder a big inheritance. You can't imagine anyone would fall for it, but they do.

When telling the World Trader story, a person will start by saying, "I heard you want to make more money." That's a great way to start, no matter who they're talking to. "Well, I came across a guy who has access to a special investment portfolio. In fact, he's one of only eight people with access, but if you put in $10,000 to $50,000, you can invest and possibly get back five, ten or fifteen times your investment."

It's a story about an amazing founder who achieved outstanding success through incredible investments, but it makes no sense. If this person had access to such amazing financial resources, why would they need to collect $10,000 to $50,000 from ordinary people?

ALTERNATIVES TO THE GURU-FOUNDER MYTH

When telling the story of your company's founder, pick two or three true facts to use as highlights. For instance, you could say, "The founder has built two existing companies doing $150 million in sales. Over the last twenty years, he's acquired a small fortune." Those two sentences are all you need. There's no reason to spruce it up, make it more exhilarating, or try to make the founder sound holy.

In the long term, a founder's reasonable, real-life success is the best possible selling point. It drives home the important message: the founder means business and will follow through on promises.

OTHER COMMON LIES ABOUT THE COMPANY

Of course, the lies told about founders ultimately lead to one of the most enticing lies: the promise of an amazing commission, which always seems to be the best in the industry. That's the lie we will examine next.

LIE

SIX

NOBODY PAYS MORE THAN WE DO

This entire industry loves to inflate numbers. I have never encountered a single company or conference that didn't inflate its numbers to some degree, and many of them take numbers that are already outstanding and double or triple them.

Nowhere is this inflation more prevalent than with commissions. The advertised commission of any particular network marketing company almost never matches the actual payout. The scenarios that are shared during pitch meetings are rarely based in reality.

I recently heard a salesperson promising a 64 percent commission. There's no possibility that anyone can earn a commission that high. By combining all sources of income, including multiple team bonuses, cars, and vacation days, it might be possible for a high-level partner to achieve somewhere between 40 and 60 percent commission, but in the beginning, it's more realistic to expect between 10 and 30 percent. In fact, that's a fair rate and can produce good money. The truth is attractive enough.

I saw this lie in action during a presentation by the American company Destiny Telecomm. As it turned out, their name was probably a bad choice, because the company's destiny was to get shut down. During their presentation, I heard them promising a 74 percent commission on long-distance calling cards. The founder claimed they were going to conquer the telecommunications world, and, at first, many people did indeed abandon their old companies and sign up with Destiny.

In reality, commissions were nowhere close to 74 percent, but the claim helped them take the market by storm. So-called experts predicted that Destiny would become the fastest-growing network marketing company the industry had ever seen. Meanwhile, the founder was pouring huge amounts of money into buying private planes and mansions. Eventually, it became clear that commissions were much lower than the promised 74 percent, and the phenomenal growth of Destiny Telecomm never materialized.

DO ANY COMPANIES PAY HIGH COMMISSIONS?

Occasionally, the high commissions companies promise are real. However, even when that's the case, it should be a warning sign. A company's balance sheet needs to add up. All the costs related to product creation, shipping, warehousing, recruitment, bonuses, and commission must add up to less than the product's price. As a result, any commission above 45 to 50 percent is probably being paid out by the company's investors and partners.

For example, on a twenty-dollar bottle of vitamin C, a commission of fourteen dollars simply isn't sustainable. You can't run a company on the remaining six dollars per bottle. If anything, the high commission is evidence that the product is inferior, or the company is fraudulent.

It's only possible to offer high commissions if the product costs very little money to produce, which is another reason for the popularity of cryptocurrencies among scammers. Since cryptocurrencies have no costs to recoup, massive commissions cost nothing. A scammer can sell a hundred-dollar token, pay a seventy-dollar commission, and still make thirty dollars in profit. In this case, high commission is nothing to brag about.

The highest commission rate I've ever seen was a claim of 76 percent from Entertainment Express. They even managed to pay the commission—for about eleven months.

Eventually the government found that they weren't producing anything. Entertainment Express was a stereotypical Ponzi scheme where established buyers were paid with money collected from new buyers. It's a money-making scheme that will always fail sooner or later, so the goal of company leaders is to make as much as possible as fast as possible before the pyramid collapses.

THE LIE ABOUT UNLIMITED DEPTH

Another traditional payment lie is *unlimited depth*, meaning if you build a team of a million people and any of them make a sale, you receive a portion of the sale—a scenario which is mathematically impossible.

Suppose I sold a product that retailed for one hundred dollars. Let's assume it cost twenty dollars to produce the product and another twenty dollars to run my business. The final sixty dollars, I offer as commission. If we pay twenty dollars for each sale, we can pay three people, max, before 100 percent of the commission will have been used, leaving nothing to pay anyone. Even if the company paid one dollar per sale, a maximum of sixty people could make this one dollar. It will never be unlimited.

At that point, I can only pay people one layer deep in my organization. As soon as another layer is recruited, I'm in the red.

If the company grows through recruitment to create a thousand layers, there are only two possibilities:

- I'm running a pyramid scam where the product increases in price with each layer, until the last layer is dealing with such an expensive product that they have no way to sell it.
- I'm running a Ponzi scheme using the money from new buyers to pay old buyers instead of producing a product, using lies about production delays when the product never shows up.

WE ARE THE ONLY ONES

Another common claim usually sounds something like this: "We're the only company offering this kind of commission plan with this specific benefit." For example, "We're the only company offering the chance to earn a free car."

Any time they are called on this lie, they simply add to it. "Sure, other companies might offer you the chance to earn a free car, but we offer the widest variety of makes and models."

In reality, almost every commission plan is duplicated numerous times by companies throughout the industry, and like most lies, this can be easily verified online.

Sometimes the promised benefit is almost impossible to obtain—more theoretical possibility than reality.

The more outlandish the benefit, the more suspect the claim. Companies love to invent catalogs of awesome rewards that partners can earn, and link them to a goal that's impossible to reach. A few companies offer private islands in exchange for $500 million in team sales, or a private jet and villa if you hit $100 million in sales a month. Frankly, if the benefit is not in reach, it's a lie.

Even if you do manage to reach a crazy sales goal, the company might simply add additional hurdles. If you reach half a billion in sales, they might come back and say, "At least 40 percent of the sales have to come from a single organization." They will find a way to keep from giving you that private island.

FASTER THAN ANYONE ELSE

Fast money is always attractive. If you type "make money" on a Google search, one of the first recommended search terms is "make money fast." Companies know this, so they like to work it into their pitches.

They might say, "If you work hard for two years, you'll make a *ton* of money." That always sounds attractive. It's certainly better than spending thirty years at a traditional job to slowly build up wealth. Many companies take this lie all the way by claiming, "You will make money faster with us than with anyone else."

In reality, the speed of income at any company depends on multiple factors, including your personality, influence, contacts, the sponsor who brought you in, and your experience, not to mention the quality of the company's product and marketing. If the company and your sponsor are exceptional, they might provide you with a bit of a shortcut, but no network marketing company can promise a single speed for making money. Too many circumstances play a role.

ZEEKREWARDS

ZeekRewards was an American company operating on a principle similar to penny stocks. Basically, their system was an online auction that let people bid tokens on cheap products. They also offered a direct investment system. One of their biggest promises was that *no one paid more*, or *paid faster*, than they did.

On the surface, their process seemed very well laid out, but I immediately saw some red flags and stayed away. Millions of people signed up with ZeekRewards before the FTC shut the whole company down. To their credit, the FTC managed to recoup some investor money, but not all of it. The founder was sentenced to nearly fifteen years behind bars.[4]

EUROPEAN KINGS CLUB

European Kings Club claimed they were destined to replace the entire banking sector. The founders still claim to this day that they were shut down because they were a threat. The truth is, they were shut down for being a Ponzi scheme.

Their pitch was, "If you have less than a million dollars in your investment portfolio, you're probably not even beating inflation, but if you invest in our community, we'll pool everyone's money into the same investment portfolio." Within the first fourteen months, they generated $1.1 billion.

In the end, the bank froze their accounts to stop them from making transfers. Leaders responded by driving their fancy cars from house to house in order to pay people their dividends in cash.[5]

As it happened, I met one of these leaders. While sitting

---

4   Associated Press, "ZeekRewards Founder Sentenced for Role in $850 Million Scam," Fox News, February 14, 2017, https://www.foxnews.com/us/zeekrewards-founder-sentenced-for-role-in-850-million-scam.

5   "European Kings Club," Wikipedia, last modification April 23, 2018, https://en.wikipedia.org/wiki/European_Kings_Club.

in his brand-new Bentley, he tried to recruit me into the company. He bragged that the trunk of his car held $160 million in cash, all of it destined to pay dividends. Of course, with no bank account and no way to transfer money, those dividends soon dried up.

PRIME BUY NETWORK

Prime Buy Network was another network marketing company that got shut down by the FTC. During their short lifetime, they told lies so brazen, it made me question humanity. At a conference, in front of 7,000 attendees, their VP of sales began shouting out the various percentage cuts people could make based on various performance benchmarks. The crowd loved it, but I sat there and added up the numbers. His percentages totaled 104 percent of the total sale price of the products. If true, then the company was actually *losing money* with every sale.

Of course, no company is in this industry to lose money, but the recruiter assumed no one in the audience would do the math. Lies like these don't even pass the common-sense test. At a bare minimum, any company leader should be able to count to a hundred when boasting about commission percentages.

WHY THESE LIES ARE USED

According to studies, most people desire to be wealthy above all else. The possibility of getting rich quick with minimal work is one of the most powerful psychological triggers a company can use, and that trigger is all the more powerful if a company offers the *only opportunity*.

Compensation is usually a combination of between five and fifteen different income streams. The money might come as a percentage of traditional retail profits, along with bonuses for recruiting a certain number of employees or increasing the size of your team. In a great company, you will also get a bonus for your success with personnel retention and performance improvement.

The easiest way to check for fraud is to add up these various income streams. In many instances, you'll find that companies can't make sense of their own numbers. Commission plans often have such complexity that it's almost impossible to figure out the actual numbers. Rules are needlessly convoluted: "You will receive a certain percentage of a certain volume of sales but only if your team is producing above a certain threshold." This complexity makes it easy for people to get lost, so they have no idea if they're being cheated.

Most people don't read their compensation plan; recruiters don't give them a chance. They get a few paragraphs in and the recruiter says something like, "This is a business based on trust. If you don't feel like you can trust us, you shouldn't join." They employ this psychological trick to dissuade people from reading the fine print.

"You've seen how impressive our founders are. You've seen the scientific evidence for our product. You know we have an advisory board. Don't you trust us?"

Once trust is established, the recruit can change all those overinflated commission percentages to less-specific promises: "Our rates are *high* and *fast*, the best in the market."

You can introduce a reality check by asking the recruiter to verify their own income, or by asking to see the back-office documents. If the recruiter says, "I made $100,000 last year," ask them how they made it. Was it split between commission and bonuses, between retail and team building, or between recruiting and education? Even if the numbers add up, it's a good idea to get clarity on the pay structure before you sign up.

INCOME STREAMS EXAMPLES	DEFINITION	NOTES
Retail Profit	Sell products to customers	
Customer Bonus	Earn money from customers re-ordering from you	
Customer Share Pool	Profit from all customer sales	Mainly for high performers
Fast Start Bonus	Make extra money by achieving your first goal fast	
Sponsor Bonus	Build the size of your team and earn money	
Team Bonus	Earn a percentage from the total sales of you team	
Rank Bonus	One-time bonus for achieving a new rank on the career ladder	
Check Match Bonus	Help your personal business partner to achieve goals and earn a percentage of the income	Usually for higher ranks in compensation plans
Car Bonus	Monthly payments for your car	Depends on the level of achievement
Annual Share Bonus	Profit share with elite leaders	

A BETTER APPROACH TO COMPENSATION

If you're pitching a compensation plan, emphasize how much it relies on performance. Give a wide but realistic range—for example, 15 to 50 percent. This establishes the right mindset, one based on *opportunity* rather than *easy money,* and it communicates that your prospect *can* make a lot of money, but they will have to *work harder* to earn more.

Fortunately, some network marketing companies have started using an honest approach. I've heard numerous ethical pitches that reveal average income based on a partner's stage on the career ladder. I like this approach because it gives people realistic sales targets for beginners. Providing average earnings for each rung of the career ladder, along with the average amount of time it takes to climb each rung, all of it backed up with data the FTC requires of companies in this industry, creates the clearest and easiest picture of potential earnings.

Pitching the company's commission in this way creates a foundation for a good-faith, long-lasting relationship, eliminating the absurdly high turnover that so many companies experience in this industry.

A good pitch might open with: "Our compensation plan pays for your efforts and rewards you for improvement. Once you build a stable business, the income will be generous."

You don't need to attach specific numbers at first. You can scare people away when you say things like, "You have the potential to make a million dollars a year." Remember, most potential recruits would be satisfied earning an extra $500 a month. Overselling doesn't help. Stay honest and focus on rewards for hard work.

HOW LONG DID IT TAKE?

Along with lies about the size or percentage of commissions, companies often exaggerate how long it took the leaders to achieve success. In the next chapters, we'll delve into forms of dishonesty about personal success.

PART TWO

LIES ABOUT YOUR SUCCESS WITH THE COMPANY

LIE
SEVEN

IT TOOK ME JUST SIX MONTHS TO HAVE THIS SUCCESS

By now you've seen that common industry lies play on well-tested psychological triggers, and they tend to follow logical flow so that one lie leads into another. This stream of exaggerated and dishonest claims includes the lies that leaders and recruiters tell about themselves.

After all, if they want to boast about the amazing wealth-making potential of their companies, they have to exaggerate their own personal success. Wildly successful people create wildly successful companies!

Leaders want to create another "wow" effect when potential recruits hear about their stories. They want people to think, "That could happen to me, too!"

I've attended thousands of conferences and sales meetings in this industry, and in my estimation, 98 percent of all leaders shorten the timeline of how long it took them to start making big money. The truth is, only one in a million experience crazy success in the shortened timelines that leaders present. It can take *many years* before leaders of successful companies can afford big homes, amazing vacations, and fancy cars.

While a leader might say, "In the first ninety days of the business, I made $50,000," they actually spent ten to fifteen years building their team, contacts, and skills. In fact, every claim of super-fast success has a hidden story about years of preparation, planning, and hard work.

Success-story lies come as easily as breathing to many leaders and recruiters because their instinct tells them to eliminate any negativity from the rousing tale. Plus, everyone does it. Lying is second nature in the industry. By the time most people learn the *real story*, they are too financially committed to leave.

THE TEARFUL PITCH

I've seen the *emotional sales pitch* more times than I care to remember. In conference after conference, I've sat and watched some poor leader get carried away by his emotions during a pitch.

He starts by bragging about his success. "After only a few months in this industry, I've experienced such wonderful results." Then he shows a slideshow of his beautiful family, his exotic vacations, his fancy cars, and maybe a few big bags of cash. The whole crowd gets whipped up into a frenzy.

At one particular conference, a recruiter from a company called ViSalus was talking about the gratitude he felt for his remarkable success. Thanks to ViSalus, he'd achieved all of his dreams after just *seven months* in the industry. The longer he spoke, the more emotional he became. Suddenly, his voice cracked, and he burst into tears. As soon as he left the stage, he was swarmed by fans.

While his fans were shaking his hand and gushing about his moving speech, a guy walked up to him and said, "I remember you. I've been coming to this conference for three years, and you've spoken at all of them. You've been doing this for years, but today, you just said you started seven months ago."

The recruiter's face turned bright red, and he stumbled through an explanation that he'd had a different sponsor in previous years.

"What I meant to say is that it's only the last seven months that really count," he said.

WHY RECRUITERS LIE ABOUT THEIR SUCCESS

I heard another recruiter claim, "I made $2,000 in the first week, and you can, too. It's easy." Of course, there is no *easy* in a new business venture. Making money requires learning and hard work. Very rarely has anyone in this industry made thousands of dollars right off the bat, and all such claims are suspect.

Lies like these are used to build a myth about the company. Sometimes, the recruiter's intentions are good. They want to inspire people and give them hope. They're trying to build up their confidence so they can hit the ground running as soon as they start. These are the recruiters who love to quote Steve Jobs and Bill Gates, college dropouts who became fabulously wealthy.

They want you to believe it could happen to you, too. While this attitude is admirable, when it becomes part of a marketing pitch, it can be exploitative. The shady recruiters know how useful these lies can be. They know these inflated promises about *how fast you can make big money* preys upon the dreams of hopeful people.

Even a recruiter who clearly hasn't been successful can use the same lies simply by creating a single degree of separation. "I only started a month ago," they might say, "but have you met Johnny? He's been here eight months, and his numbers are incredible."

Many potential recruits would be perfectly happy enjoying modest success after two years of hard work, and if that was the pitch, they would buy in right away. However, most recruiters sidestep the long-term commitment. "Two years? Are you crazy? You'll have all the success you ever wanted in nine months!"

SPOTTING THE LIE

When a recruiter starts talking about how fast they got rich, you can uncover the lie fairly quickly. Ask to see the fancy car. The recruiter might be financing the car, but even then, they must have a respectable income and good credit to finance an expensive vehicle. It verifies at least some aspect of their story.

A more effective approach is to ask about their experience with other companies. Ask if they came to their current company with a team already in place. Chances are, they will be excited to brag, and they might get carried away telling the truth. If they do, they will soon reveal that their sudden success was actually the result of many *years* of hard work and experience in the industry.

Attending big events and conferences often reveals if a company has a culture of dishonesty. If you see multiple leaders on stage boasting about how quickly they achieved success, while the newbies are sitting in the audience struggling, you know something's wrong.

Some people have been in this industry so long that they repeat stories they've heard from other people as if it were their own. They've drunk so much network marketing Kool-Aid they can no longer limit themselves to reality. It's practically a cult mentality.

THE HONEST ALTERNATIVE

There's no reason not to be *crystal clear* about the relationship between time and success. Everything in life has a learning curve, and no reasonable person expects to achieve huge success without investing some time and effort.

It's perfectly fine to brag, as long as you're bragging about the truth. Don't be afraid to share actual success stories. Sometimes, we under-promise and over-deliver, and you don't want to do that either.

Most of the time, however, recruiters do the opposite. Success is always *easy* and *fast*, but when you tell someone, "Anyone can achieve success in six months with our program," you set people up to fail. Most people won't experience that kind of success. Like almost every job in the world, a network marketing job takes years to master.

Somehow, in this industry, people think there are short-cuts. There are *no shortcuts*. Overnight success simply doesn't happen.

Instead of lying, it's better to manage people's expectations. Like with anything else, new recruits must take baby steps at first. To help them do this, explain the company culture, then explain the product and key highlights of the compensation plan, and finally, present a plan of action that realistically portrays how the new recruit fits into the team, taking into account their experience and level of influence. This is called "framing."

The right frame allows you to shake hands and make a real commitment. The new recruit will understand the need to invest time and effort. Ultimately, it's better and easier to tell the truth.

The good news is, in this industry, the truth is mostly positive. Real success is possible with many companies if people put in the time and effort. Anyone can earn a decent income, but working an hour a week and making big money is impossible. On the other hand, with the right company, you might start working ten hours a week and make decent money, in time.

The truth is less intimidating. It sounds *attainable*. When people make insane promises, potential recruits get scared rather than motivated. It undermines their will to learn. There's just no advantage to lying.

Instead, explain why some people go through the ranks quickly, while most newbies won't. Then ask the recruit what they personally want to achieve and tailor your pitch based on their response.

EVERYONE IS EQUAL

Not only do company leaders boast that success can come insanely fast, but they also like to promise that everyone who is new to the company starts in an equal position. While this makes it sound like a *fair fight*, it's almost never the truth, as we will see.

LIE
EIGHT

EVERYONE STARTS
AT THE SAME PLACE

If success is a competition, we all just want a level playing field, and that's exactly what this industry promises. It's a fair fight, and you have the same chance as anyone else to be healthy, wealthy, and happy, regardless of your age, background, education, gender, or experience.

To be fair, I think this lie is closer to the truth in our industry than in most others. Generally speaking, a company's compensation plan will pay the same no matter who you are. However, there are numerous factors that give beginners in this industry unequal footing, some of which can even eliminate the opportunity altogether.

I've fallen for this lie before and lost. Early in my career, it destroyed my confidence in the industry. My first experience working with multilevel marketing was a company called HMI in Hamburg, Germany. Their sales division told me, "Everyone enters the business on equal footing," and I fell for it hard.

For once, life seemed to be offering me a completely fair fight, and I signed up. I worked as hard as I could, sixteen hours a day, seven days a week, trying to achieve the dream. After three and a half years, I'd worked my way into the top 1,500 out of 100,000 partners in the company. As a reward, I was invited to a special seminar for company leaders in Switzerland taught by a famous professor.

At the seminar, I met and chatted with other participants about how amazing it was to achieve success, and everyone agreed with me and responded with excitement. Then I spoke to a woman sitting beside me. I asked her about the sacrifices she'd had to make to reach this level of success—the years of hard work, losing friends, skipping holidays.

She gave me a confused look. "Years of hard work?" she said. "What are you talking about? I started at this rank."

"That's not possible," I replied. "The company philosophy is that everyone starts at the same place. That's the reason for HMI's success. We've jumped over the biggest gap, from sales rep to team management."

She insisted her story was true. She had started at this level.

Needing to know the truth, I stood up and interrupted the speaker on stage. I told him the woman's story and asked if it was true. The whole room erupted in chaos.

Sheepishly, the speaker admitted that the woman's story was true. Some people—a select few—did indeed start at a higher level.

The next day, still furious, I canceled my contract with the company. I probably should have thought about it a bit longer, because canceling my contract also canceled my income, but I felt like a fool. I'd fallen for a blatant lie and the company hadn't even tried that hard to cover it up.

At the time, I was a student with no business experience. The woman at the conference was an insurance agent with twenty-five years of experience. Though she had no direct marketing experience, she was able to make big promises based on her track record, so the company decided to place her in one of the top positions in their compensation plan—a position that would normally have taken years to achieve.

Though it might not sound like a big deal, it destroyed the ethical foundation on which the company built its sales pitch. There was no equal footing for new recruits. Some people were given a distinct advantage over others. Sadly, this happens quite often behind the scenes throughout this industry.

MOVING LEGS BEHIND THE SCENES

No matter what companies promise, if you have experience in a related industry, the higher-ups often want to profit from your presence, so they grandfather you in on top of the existing business, placing you in a higher-than-usual starting position in the compensation plan (often above an existing team of distributors who are already producing sales).

Even if this is common practice, it's absolutely devastating to young recruits who have sacrificed years to climb the ladder on a promise of *fair play*. Finding out, once you've reached a higher rank in the company, that some people got an express elevator to the top floor makes all of that work feel like a scam.

Even worse, rather than having to build their own team, these "select few" might be handed a preexisting team worth $100,000 a month or more on day one. I have heard of cases where entire national organizations were gifted to new recruits with the right experience. It's essentially a bribe meant to draw in big-time talent, and it wouldn't be a big deal if it didn't go against the promises most companies make.

Another incentive companies use is called "moving legs." If one of these superstars is grandfathered into team management from day one, there's a good chance they will lose some of the existing team members or clients. Under normal circumstances, these losses would cause the individual to lose rank. To prevent this, companies will shift team members or clients around, "moving legs" in order to bolster the failing team so the superstar new recruit maintains their rank.

Sadly, this is a common practice meant to keep superstars from moving to a different company. Companies as diverse as Herbalife, Intel Communications, and Entertainment Express have used this "moving legs" strategy relentlessly to insulate their core leaders during tough times.

MY EXPERIENCE BEING OFFERED TEAMS

I'm no longer an inexperienced new recruit. Having worked in this industry for many years with an established and solid track record, I attract many lucrative offers from self-proclaimed headhunters.

Jeunesse, the skincare company, tried to recruit me by guaranteeing an incoming of $45,000 a month for two years. They sent me a proposal in which they offered me an existing team, assuring me that I would only need about 25 percent of a normal workload to meet my sales requirement. Along with the income and team, they promised a whole range of perks.

First Investment Group, a rather well-known European company, also tried to recruit me by offering control of an organization that was already selling $60 million a year. I had done a bit of work with the company in the past, so they wanted me to come in and train the organization, reaping massive benefits from day one.

These offers were so attractive, only an idiot would say no. I admit I thought long and hard about accepting them. I'm as susceptible to temptation as anyone, but in the end, I turned them down because of the ethical dilemma. Maybe the old wounds from HMI had never healed, but I didn't want to be in a position to devastate some bright-eyed, hard-working new recruit.

Also, I didn't want the bad karma. What goes around comes around. I believe that, and I try to live that way.

From a practical perspective, these kinds of grandfa-thering deals chase away new recruits and damage the whole industry. Nobody should start with an unearned position or accept a company handout. It goes against the foundational ethics of the industry, breeds jealousy, and destroys morale.

WHY THIS LIE IS USED

Every business, university, and professional sports team wants to recruit high performers in order to gain an advantage over the competition. The easiest way to do this is to offer the superstar recruit a sweeter deal, rewarding them for past experience.

When a promising new company appears on the scene, hype builds quickly. People in the industry begin to whisper, "Hey, these guys might be the next big thing." As a result, experienced distributors who are unhappy with their current companies begin to consider making a move. Leaving behind an established team is never easy, so new companies want to do whatever they can to make the transition smooth.

By doing this, companies also create apparent evidence of impossible success stories. When someone is secretly grandfathered in, it looks to potential new recruits like they achieved huge success in a very short period of time.

"Wow, you really *can* make money fast at this company," they think. "That person has only worked here for a month, and they've already reached the highest level."

The grandfathered superstar becomes a symbol of the company's potential, a recruitment tool to entice the hopeful.

There are some legitimate quick-success stories where new recruits with particular insight have done well in record time, but they are the exception. Companies in every sector of this industry are notorious for paying secret up-front bonuses, and "moving legs" to grandfather in experienced people, and the most infamous example is the company that approached me, Jeunesse.

One of their top leaders was given multiple organizations within the company in order to create and maintain his legendary success story. He and his wife are a "power couple" at the company, two successful, good-looking people who seem to confirm every inflated promise of success.

Another famous example of grandfathering happened at Lyoness. When their top leader stumbled, the company gave her the sales team for an entire country, making her the exclusive business manager of the territory under the guise that she had earned it, all so they could continue celebrating her supposed "amazing achievements."

Naturally, all of these grandfathered leaders know they've been given a rare gift that has nothing to do with their actual achievements at the company. It is clearly a handout, but it makes them dependent on the founder's support. If anything, these superstar recruits will be less likely to complain or try to change anything at the company because of the implied threat from the founder: "Do you want me to reveal how much I've given to you?"

In time, these special recruits begin buying their own press, telling their own trumped-up story of swift success so often that they believe it.

HOW TO SPOT THE LIE

Of the lies in this book, this one is the hardest to uncover. When a professional sports team makes a lucrative trade, it can be very difficult to learn the full details of that trade. Managers like to keep such deals between themselves.

In a similar way, network marketing companies won't readily reveal when they've sweetened the deal to bring in a special recruit. However, if a company shares unbelievable success stories, it's a good idea to assume they might be putting their thumb on the scale. The only way to confirm this is to talk to some of these fast-rising leaders. Ask them directly if they brought their team with them from another company. If you catch them off guard, they might accidentally give you an honest answer.

IS IT ALL BAD?

In sports, a superstar athlete like Michael Jordan would never move to a new team if he had to start all over as a rookie. The good news is, even a new recruit can reach the superstar level someday. If you make a name for yourself, become a top leader, create good teams with high retention rates, and gain knowledge in a valuable niche, you will *earn* equal footing with the Michael Jordans of network marketing.

This is simply how the game is played—not just in network marketing, but in every industry. Headhunters in the corporate world are always looking for superstars. If you have a strong track record in sales, a headhunter will almost certainly offer you a better package than a guy fresh out of college.

Look at the unequal footing as motivation to become the best you can be, and one day, you might become a superstar yourself.

Sadly, there's not much else you can do. With this lie, we sometimes have to fall back on the old Serenity Prayer:

"God, grant me the serenity to accept the things I cannot change, the courage to change the things I can, and the wisdom to know the difference."

Just know that unequal treatment happens, no matter what companies claim. There's nothing you can do to stop it. If you want to become a successful leader at a network marketing company, you will simply have to run a few unfair races in your career.

I still remember how I felt at that moment in Switzerland when I realized I had been lied to. The pain lingered a long time. This particular lie hurts, but there's not much that can be done to stop it. Do the best you can to compete and focus on the positive side of the business.

WHAT TO SAY INSTEAD

My advice to recruiters is *always be honest*. Tell new recruits the truth, and you will avoid creating disillusionment. There's simply no reason to keep promoting this lie that everyone starts at the same place.

If you don't know your company's philosophy about this, don't bring it up during recruitment discussions. You won't harm your chances by telling a potential recruit that early success depends largely on circumstances. Avoid theoretical success stories that can become sources of discouragement later.

If asked about unequal starting positions, admit it. You can even say, "It's just common sense to entice experienced people to join the company, but the good news is, you have the chance to get where they are in time." However, if they don't ask directly, it's better not to bring it up at all. In fact, as we often say in sales, "Don't provoke foolish questions from customers by making unnecessary comments about something that doesn't matter in the first place."

Instead, emphasize the positive. Explain that the business model allows everyone to be paid the same commission on the same products. Additionally, reinforce the fact that individuals ultimately determine their own career growth. Above all, encourage recruits to focus on their own story instead of the stories of others.

OTHER LIES ABOUT SUCCESS

The lie that everyone starts at the same place is often tied to the false promise that every recruit receives a massive amount of support. Companies and sponsors love to promise potential recruits that they will hold their hand every step of the way.

They won't.

LIE

NINE

YOU'RE IN IT *FOR* YOURSELF, BUT NOT *BY* YOURSELF

The title of this chapter is a famous quote in this industry. Of all the lies in this book, I hate this one the most, and people who have been scammed by it will almost certainly agree. Unlike some of the lies, this one is unforgivably *mean* because it kills people's dreams.

Joining this industry in the beginning felt a lot like my first day of university. Campus was huge. I was surrounded by buildings with a thousand different doors I could enter. People were moving in all directions, and I felt overwhelmed—both with *possibility* and with *responsibility*.

I had to find my classes and figure out what was going on. If someone had come up to me, shook my hand, and said, "Welcome to university. I'm here to help you find your classes, gather your books and supplies, and meet new friends for lunch," I would have been immensely grateful.

In a perfect world, we would all have someone to help us overcome obstacles, and to a certain degree, we all hope for it. That's why this lie is so cruel. Even if you're an experienced and successful entrepreneur, you still need help navigating new situations. You want someone to take your hand and show you the way.

"I'm here to help. We'll do this together. You're never alone. I will walk with you step by step to make sure you're successful."

That promise is made constantly throughout the network marketing industry, but in almost every instance, the harsh reality hits not long after new recruits sign up and commit some money. Once leaders get their cut for recruiting a new member, they knock the dust off their shoes and say, "Well, now it's up to them."

To a certain extent, this is a fair attitude. Everyone should take responsibility for their own success. In a race, no runner should expect to be carried from the starting line.

Again, the real problem here is the vast gulf between what leaders promise and what they deliver. Often, the difference is presented in a subtle way. Before new recruits sign on the dotted line, they are told, "I will hold your hand every step of the way." After new recruits sign on the dotted line, this promise becomes, "I told you I'll be here for you, so just call me any time you need help."

Leaders might even use the old saying, often misattributed to the Buddha, "When the student is ready, the teacher will appear." What they mean by this is, "When you get to a certain level of skill, I'll help you."

New recruits don't completely give up hope at this point, because they can tell themselves, "Well, I just have to get some initial momentum going, and then they will come in and help me." However, in most cases, the teacher never appears. New recruits were on their own from day one—they just didn't know it.

At the same time, if you don't know which classes to attend, what school supplies you need, or how to prepare, you will never be ready. It becomes a chicken-or-egg situation.

"The student is never ready, so the teacher never appears. The teacher never appears, so the student is never ready."

THE IMPACT OF POOR SUPPORT

In the network marketing industry, the biggest problem is

attrition: people leaving companies, most often because of a lack of support. If attrition decreased, the industry would have a better reputation and higher profits.

In my experience, I estimate that 70 to 90 percent of new business partners quit in the first month of joining a network marketing company. The big dream of a fancy new car or just a few hundred dollars a month dies fast. People learn almost immediately that network marketing doesn't offer easy money, and that $10,000 a month they were promised just isn't there.

They could earn that much money in time, but with little to no support, they can't gain any traction. Feeling hopeless, they chalk it up to a lesson learned and walk away.

Additionally, the recruiter's many lies soon become clear, so new recruits decide they don't want to associate with a liar. The company appears to promote liars into places of leadership, which absolutely eradicates their integrity.

What a terrible way to grow a business, much less an industry.

WE'RE A FAMILY

Have you ever heard a recruit say, "We're not a business— we're a family"? Maybe you've said it yourself.

WHERE DO LEADERS LEARN TO TELL THESE LIES?

There is no book that explicitly instructs leaders and recruiters to lie. "Use Lie X to make people sign up, Lie Y to make them stick around, and Lie Z to make them spend more money." That information isn't contained in any official training materials.

Instead, people adopt these lies instinctively as they see others being rewarded for them. Since the more successful leaders lie constantly, the culture encourages it.

"I want to become as successful at the superstars," recruits say, "so I'd better do what they do."

These lies spread like viruses, infecting whole companies, and they're very hard to cure. The business press pours fuel on the fire by trumpeting success stories with so-called "reviews."

For example, the company Business For Home is run by self-proclaimed multilevel marketing experts who review various MLM and network marketing companies. Their website includes a "top income" list that shows the name, income, and company of the industry's most financially successful people. However, any time a new company appears in the industry, their leaders dominate most of the entries on the top income list.

Anyone reading the website would think, "Wow, that new company is creating so many success stories. They must provide a lot of support." However, the opposite is almost always true. The initial burst of success doesn't last.

In some cases, as with OneCoin, the founder soon disappears, and the Business For Home website is forced to publish a retraction: "Due to the disappearance of the founder, we have decided to remove all names associated with the company."

By then, it's too late. Many people have already signed up based largely on the website's supposed research. They've lost their money, and no retraction can bring it back.

This virus spreads fast and digs in deep, but I like to think of this book as a vaccine. At the very least, I hope readers will discover in these pages a better, more honest, and more rewarding way of doing business.

It's a comforting lie. After all, family is always there for you. They remain your family in good times and bad. If you ask for help, they will give it. Blood is thicker than water. Isn't that what they say?

However, someone claiming to be family shouldn't be trying to smooth-talk you into buying more products or signing up for expensive events. I like to tell people, "If the company was my family, then I'd rather stay single."

To be fair, there are some companies that do treat members like family. They go the extra mile and work hard to build strong relationships. However, they comprise, at most, 5 to 10 percent of the industry. They are the exception, not the rule. If you have found a team, sponsor, or people who care, you're better off staying where you are and making it work—it might be the only time it will happen in your entire life!

WE WORK TOGETHER

A related lie plays off the idea of being a family. It usually goes something like this: "Since I'm always going to be there for you, I'll help you put together your team."

Nothing is more intimidating for a potential recruit than the idea of building their initial team from nothing, so this version of the support lie creates a very effective recruitment bribe. If the recruiter follows through, then there's no problem, but often they don't.

It's always wrong to create a mindset that people will be *given* something rather than *earn* it. Imagine a French teacher promising a new student, "I will implant half the French language in your brain. You will only have to study and learn the other half." It wouldn't take that student long to figure out the promise was a lie.

CREATING A VICIOUS CYCLE

With the support lie, leaders wind up teaching people to be dependent and reactive. A company isn't a family, no matter what leaders say. It is a professional work environment, even if the leaders are fun and friendly. Hard work is essential.

Leaders create a vicious cycle. To get people to sign up, they tell them to relax. "It's easy. We'll hold your hand."

Believing the lie, new recruits come on board and immediately become inactive, waiting for someone to hold their hand. Then leaders turn right around and complain to one another that their team members are lazy.

All of this could be avoided if leaders just told the truth.

HOW TO SPOT THE LIE

Spotting this lie takes a bit of detective work. Ask recruiters to share a few stories about how they've supported new team members in the past, and request the actual names of team members they've helped. If those team members corroborate the story, then there might be some truth to the company's promise.

Bear in mind, when you attempt to talk to a team member to corroborate a recruiter's story, you are likely to get any number of excuses as to why they can't speak with you. They might be on vacation, or they might be "really busy" with the business. Don't give up. Be persistent. You need to speak to a team member before you accept a promise of support from a leader.

Sometimes, the leader won't be able to provide you with a reference. To avoid having to do so, they might share a story unrelated to their own team.

"Let me tell you what one of our other leaders did for their team members."

Human psychology works against you. When leaders use Facebook, they'll often "like" their team's status updates, so it seems like they are involved and supportive. Even if team members aren't getting the support they need, they tend to like the leader—another aspect of the cult mentality in network marketing.

To unmask this lie, find someone raving about a leader (perhaps on social media, or possibly in person) and ask for specifics.

"How has the leader helped you? How much time have they committed to you?"

Request specifics. If they can't provide them, that's a red flag.

A BETTER APPROACH TO OFFERING SUPPORT

The most frequent bit of advice I give to leaders is, "Don't say you will do it if you won't do it." If you can't provide the level of support you claim to provide, don't make the promise. Think before you speak, and if you accidentally promise too much, live up to the commitment.

It's that simple.

I understand, sometimes people get excited and make promises they can't keep. When you're close to recruiting someone, it's easy to take it a little too far. Suddenly, without intending to, you told them you'd assist with their first ten calls.

Don't go back on it. Assist with those calls, use the experience as a self-coaching opportunity, and be more careful in the future about the promises you make. Never ever fail to provide the support you said you'd provide. If you promise mentorship, you must deliver. Anything less is cruel.

Whatever you promise or don't promise, I strongly encourage you to call each team member regularly and guide them toward activities that provide opportunities for personal and professional growth. Some degree of mentorship should be the industry standard. Book appointments together. Schedule presentations together. Attend meetings together.

This is the bare minimum for a *good* trainer. If you can't provide enough training and support to ensure new recruits do their jobs well, you shouldn't be recruiting. Training is the only real quality assurance for your company, or for the industry as a whole.

Just because you told someone how to do their job and they said, "Okay, I got it," doesn't mean you're off the hook. You must see how they apply instructions, with your own eyes. Consider your role as similar to a sports coach. A coach doesn't tell a player what to do one time and then sit in their office. They observe the player on the field so they can spot mistakes.

If that sounds like too much work, then at least tell people up front you don't provide mentoring. "You're on your own." Believe it or not, self-motivated, driven recruits respond well to this. Some people love the challenge.

On the other hand, if a potential recruit is hesitant about learning and building a business on their own, you either need to find someone on your team who can provide training or just don't sign that recruit up.

Offering mentorship is an individual commitment. With each and every recruit, before you shake hands and offer help, consider whether you truly have the time to follow through.

You must tell the truth, even if it's not what a recruit wants to hear. For example, you might say, "I understand you want me to come to meetings every day, but I can only support you twice a week due to the pressures of my corporate job. I do this part-time, just like you. Still, you can reach out to other team members if you need daily support."

With this approach, there are no secrets or surprises. A new partner can't complain that you failed to live up to your commitments.

OTHER COMMON LIES ABOUT SUCCESS

Along with offering amazing support, many companies also try to make the work sound as simple and easy as possible. Everyone dreams of achieving success with minimal work, so this lie works well for recruitment, as we will see.

LIE

TEN

IT'S SO SIMPLE, ANYONE CAN DO IT

If a job sounds too hard, people won't do it. As a result, industry leaders tend to downplay the amount of time new recruits need to spend training, learning, and applying new skills to be successful.

The truth should be obvious: this industry, like most industries, demands hard work.

Sadly, many companies entice new recruits with the claim, "This job is so simple, anyone can do it." There might be a grain of truth in the lie. Some network marketing tasks are indeed quite simple. However, to truly develop a reliable income stream and turn it into a career, people have to work very hard and commit a lot of time. The journey to big success takes many years, as with any other career.

WHY DON'T YOU FIX YOUR TEETH?

I once attended a conference in which a friend's rude comment almost derailed a recruiter's presentation. The man onstage claimed that his company's product would allow any vehicle to run three times as long on gas fumes when the tank was empty.

It was a ridiculous claim, as stupid as the magic washing machine ball from chapter two.

"Selling this product is so simple, anyone can do it," the man said. "Anyone can make a massive amount of money in a very short period of time."

As he spoke, I noticed the man was missing his two front teeth. My friend noticed as well, and he raised his hand to ask a question.

"If everything is so simple, and anyone can make a massive amount of money," he asked, "why haven't you paid to fix your teeth?"

Everyone in the room gasped, and I cringed. It was bad form, but perhaps he made a relevant point. Still, I prefer to unmask lies less aggressively.

A STUPID SALES PITCH

I was already running a successful investment business when a salesman from the National Safety Associates gave me a very unusual pitch.

He told me I was *stupid*.

I had already explained to him that I worked sixteen hours a day, six days a week, and he seemed offended.

"Why would you work so hard? That's stupid. Working *less* is what network marketing is all about. You decide when, where, and with whom you work. I'm successful because I relax. I don't sell, I *share*. Nobody wants to sell."

The last sentence was true. Few jobs have less prestige than sales.

The recruiter from the network marketing company continued: "Everyone drinks water. Everyone breathes air. Wouldn't you agree that it's important to have clean water and air? I can come over right now and show you how easy it is."

I was curious enough to let the guy come over, and soon, he showed up at my door. He chatted a bit to warm me up, then he produced a water filter and went to the kitchen to install it in my sink.

Immediately, he ran into a problem. The filter was supposed to attach to the end of the faucet, but it didn't fit, and the salesman didn't have the right adapter. The guy was persistent, however, and eventually he made it fit anyway.

Then he turned on the faucet and asked me to taste the water. I got a glass, filled it, and took a big swig. I couldn't taste any difference.

"But can you at least see how simple this job is?" he replied.

"Not really," I said. "I just watched you spend almost an hour trying to install a water filter that didn't affect the taste of the water. Still, if it's so simple, you must be enjoying great success."

"Yeah, I am," he said. "Of course."

"Do you have any documents about the business?"

"In the car," he said.

In the olden days, the way to discover if someone was successful was to check their watch, car, and teeth. I didn't really want to see his company's documents. I wanted to see what kind of car he was driving.

As he stepped outside, I spotted it—an old Volkswagen

van in terrible condition. It was parked very close to my brand-new Porsche.

"I'll be honest with you," I said. "I'm a salesperson. I love selling. I know most people don't like it, but I do. I believe in selling. Judging by the condition of the vehicle you parked in front of my house today, I have to say, it doesn't look like everyone can succeed with your company."

Ducking his head, he agreed with me.

HOW TO LEARN THE REQUISITE SKILLS

Network marketing is never simple. You have to learn the skills to make it work, and the best way to learn is to find a mentor, preferably a mentor who is still actively working in the industry. The old saying is true in network marketing: "Those who can, do; those who can't, teach."

Find a mentor with experience. Business courses are no substitute for industry success, and too many trainers provide a purely informative, even academic, approach to the business. The *how* is often missing. I've seen this in countless training courses. Fantastic speakers get on stage and pump up the crowd, getting everyone excited and saying all the right things, but they skim over the *how*. As a result, people walk away unsure how to apply what they've learned.

THE EDUCATION LIE

Sometimes, lies about simplicity are tied to promises of thorough education. Many companies even offer training programs to back up this claim, but most don't. However, the programs typically focus on having the right attitude and proper motivation. They hardly touch on actual skills development.

A company should teach new recruits to identify their ideal customer. What does the ideal customer want? Where are they found? Who are the allies that can help make connections? How can you approach those allies? Without the skills to answer these questions, new recruits have to depend on luck.

Another skill every company should teach is *presentation*. It takes skill to deliver a pitch that will lead to a follow-up appointment. Every medium—email, phone, social media—requires its own approach, and learning these skills takes constant practice.

When you present the business, you can't be too direct. You can't walk into a meeting and say, "Hello, how are you? Let me tell you about the business." You have to learn how to develop empathy, how to warm up a crowd, and once the presentation begins, you must demonstrate enough knowledge and authority to close the deal. Rarely does this come naturally to a new recruit.

Making a sale requires understanding the *psychology* of the sales process. I've had people say to me, "In my country, we have a different culture. People won't fall for that here."

I always reply, "Then you're surrounded by nonhumans."

Sales psychology is *human* psychology. If you understand how humans think and react, you can make a sale, but it requires a lot of training.

Closing a sale isn't even the end. Properly closing a sale leads to recommendations for new opportunities, but obtaining those recommendations is an art. Most people can't pull off the line, "Can you give me the names of ten other people who would like to try this product?" They need to learn how to relate the value of the customer's purchase to their circle of influence.

Once a new recruit masters all of the above skills, the company should start training them in leadership. Although some core elements stay the same, leadership at each level of scale is very different, so leadership training should be ongoing.

None of this is *simple.*

EVERYONE SAYS YES

"It's simple because everyone will say yes." I've heard that lie many times. Why will everyone say yes to the product? Because they need it. Remember, everyone drinks water, so of course they need an expensive filter that takes an hour to attach to the faucet in order to provide clean water that tastes exactly the same. It's so simple.

This lie falls apart with just a little common sense. Everyone does indeed need clean water, but "clean water" doesn't automatically mean "subscription to a water filter service."

In fact, common sense alone tells us that there is *no single product* that makes everyone in the world say yes. Apple is the most valuable brand in the world, and many people feel like they need an iPhone, but not me. I don't need an Android phone either. Believe it or not, I'm a dinosaur that still pines for Blackberry. Consequently, if some salesperson promised the whole world a cheap upgrade from a Blackberry phone to an iPhone, I wouldn't say yes.

CREATING AN ANGRY MOB

People who fall for the lies in this chapter rarely do well in this industry. Eventually, they fail and join the ever-increasing mob of angry former recruits saying terrible things about network marketing.

"I was told it was so simple anyone could do it," they might say, "but I pitched to fifty different people and didn't make a single sale. This industry is full of liars. They told me I could make tons of money, but all I did was *lose* money paying for the products and a few training courses."

The water filter salesman told me, in the middle of his pitch, "You don't have to sell anything. We show people our filters, and eight out of ten say yes."

I first heard a version of this lie at HMI when a leader told me, "Selling our product is like walking into a mall and just handing someone the keys to your car. 'Here you go. Take my car. It's free.' Who wouldn't love that?"

Being the curious person I am, I decided to try it. I went to a shopping mall, pulled out the key to my car, and tried to give the car to someone. I approached the first friendly person I saw and said, "Excuse me. You look like a positive person. I've had a fantastic day. Please take the key to my car. It's an Audi 80. It's not in perfect shape, but it's a good car. It'll get you home."

I tried this dozens of times, and I didn't get a single taker.

Even though I was offering it for free, people were skeptical. We all know nothing is life is truly free. When someone makes a crazy offer that appears to cost nothing, we always wonder, "What's the catch?"

If a free car doesn't interest everyone, no product pitch is going to interest everyone in the world. Common sense alone tells you that.

SORTING, NOT SELLING

A similar marketing lie goes like this: "It's sorting, not selling."

In other words, all you have to do is present the opportunity, and people will decide if it's right for them. It's *that simple.*

While there's a small amount of truth to this, in reality, you still need to close every deal. There's always a process to selling, even if you find a potential recruit who is motivated and hungry for success. In that case, you are competing with other companies providing similar opportunities. With network marketing, thousands of companies are out there selling, lying, promising, and bribing to drive people into their businesses.

A salesperson can use hard facts and a winning personality, but they still have to *sell*, and doing it well requires learning how to communicate the value you deliver.

HOW TO SPOT THE LIE

With all of these simplicity lies, my favorite approach is to ask the liar to demonstrate how easy their job is. Most meetings happen in hotel foyers, since companies don't want to pay for meeting rooms, so there are usually ample opportunities for a recruiter or salesperson to demonstrate their sales technique.

"This sounds interesting," I might say. "The process you've describes really does seem simple. Would you mind approaching a few of the strangers around us and showing me just how simple it is to get a *yes*?"

Then I will point to a few specific people.

This is where the fun begins. Some recruiters give up immediately because they don't actually pitch to customers. Others attempt it, but it's almost always awkward. Since the process is never simple, most of these attempts end badly.

In fact, I've seen a few salespeople, desperate to back up their lie, get so aggressive trying to show me their process that they came close to getting punched in the face.

WHAT TO SAY INSTEAD

I keep saying it. Always be honest!

A good recruit enjoys a challenge, so there's no need to make the job sound simple. Most people understand that there's a learning curve, and it takes time to learn new skills.

Tell the truth, and follow it up by saying, "Isn't it great to add another skillset to your repertoire?"

Explain how helpful sales skills can be in daily life. Joke about how selling will help the recruit in the next argument with their spouse.

Present your business in this way:

"This business isn't simple. It requires constant learning. As we grow, we need to learn different skills. I want to take you through it one step at a time. After every achievement, we will discuss what you have learned and how it applies to the next stage."

Don't overdo it. You certainly don't need to say, "This is the hardest challenge you've ever faced. Most people aren't smart enough to do it."

That approach is neither true nor helpful. In my experience, of the people who are willing to put in the time and effort, about 80 percent will achieve a solid five-figure income.

If the recruit seems willing, even eager, to invest the time and effort to learn, then you've found a great team member.

OTHER COMMON LIES ABOUT EASE

Not only is the business so simple anyone can do it, but according to many company leaders, anyone can make big money working part-time. Making a million dollars a year for part-time work certainly sounds enticing, but it's the next lie we must confront.

LIE
ELEVEN

YOU CAN MAKE BIG MONEY WORKING PART-TIME

"Making money is easy" isn't a strong enough lie for some companies. They have to take it a little farther.

The recruiters love to use a specific tactic. Instead of selling you on the product, they say, "All I need is your contact list. I will introduce the product to everyone on your behalf, and you can enjoy *passive income.*"

Let me be blunt. Any promise of "passive income" in this industry is a lie from start to finish. Anyone foolish enough to believe it won't last more than a couple of months. Most people abuse the term "passive income" based on a limited understanding of the meaning. What they are referring to is actually "recurring income," in which a portion of your income is likely to continue even without selling to new clients.

A real passive income requires a lot of active work over a number of years to generate. Anyone claiming you can make passive income is probably a new recruit. They've failed to achieve any success, so they're becoming desperate. This lie is their last-ditch attempt to suck someone, anyone, into the business. Since they lack the skillset to build a business, they can't make good on the promise anyway.

The softer version of "passive income" is "part-time income," which is usually attached to huge sums of money.

"You can become filthy rich working part-time."

I've heard that lie more times than I can recount. Sometimes, a specific dollar amount is attached to the lie.

"You could make as much as $10,000 a month with just a few hours of work every week."

THE TRUTH ABOUT PART-TIME

As with everything in life, you get out what you put in. Your earnings *always* correlate with your weekly hours, so the more time you spend learning and applying skills and remaining persistent, the higher your income will be.

You can make a profit working part-time, but there is no

industry where a few hours a week will generate a ton of money. Realistically, you might make around $500 a month working a few hours a week, assuming the product and company are good. That's nothing to sneeze at, but it's not a path to becoming a millionaire.

It's even possible to generate $1,000 a month working part-time, but it won't happen in the first few months. Sharing the product and following up with customers day in and day out, month in and month out, might eventually get you there, but you are very unlikely to ever get rich.

The idea that a sponsor can provide you with a passive income is far too good to be true. The dream scenario of sitting at home, waiting for the bank to call and ask why so much money is flowing into your account, simply doesn't happen.

I have sympathy for people who fall for this lie. It's only human to want an easy path to wealth, happiness, and ease. Sometimes, the unfulfilled desire overwhelms common sense.

SUCCESS TAKES A LONG TIME

When I first jumped into this industry, I went all the way. I fell in love with the possibility of making unlimited money, so I quit university and went all in. Initially,

I'd plan to take a one-semester break, but I never went back, devoting myself to marketing full-time. In the early years, I made as many mistakes in this industry as there are mistakes to make, but my insane level of persistence kept me going. Over time, I learned from my mistakes and honed my skills, but I endured many setbacks along the way.

The first company I worked for, HMI, drew me in with their slogan: "We're not just selling insurance; we're financing the future."

Sadly, after I signed up, my HMI sponsor provided no support. He essentially abandoned me as soon as he had my signature on the contract. I could have given up, but that's not my style. Instead, I decided to get revenge.

I began learning the skills I needed on my own, and I worked constantly. The first year went horribly. I looked at other recruiters and salespeople in the company and saw a bunch of people with no academic background. I assumed I would outperform them, but after eleven months, my total income was $474. I'd spent all my savings and made almost nothing while working sixteen hours a day, seven days a week.

I didn't give up. I knew other people were making good money, and I was determined to join them.

Everything took a sudden, dramatic turn in my twelfth month. I still remember the moment the company sent me my check that month, and I saw the dollar amount: $10,640. I couldn't believe it.

I drove immediately to the bank and asked the teller to cash the check, so I could hold it in my hand and know it was real. I had worked so hard for so long, but all of that hard work and learning had finally paid off. It didn't arrive passively, and it didn't come through part-time work. I worked very hard and *earned it*.

HOW TO SPOT THE PART-TIME LIE

When it comes to exaggerated claims of part-time success, you will always get the truth by checking back office documents. If a recruiter claims to make $60,000 a month, first, congratulate them. Then, ask to see documents showing those sales. Every company tracks these numbers, so pulling up a document to prove a salesperson's income should be easy.

You can also create a breakdown of their hours. If someone claims to make big money working part-time, ask them how many personal meetings they attend, how many cities they visit, and how many clients they pitch to in an average week. Give them a chance to brag about how hard they work. Most people love to brag, so they will say, "I have businesses in six cities. I drive back and forth all the time. I conduct ten meetings a week." Chances are, you'll discover they spend very little time watching TV and texting while the money rolls in.

In direct marketing, many activities are routine. You have a core workload you must get through every week. When you know what the core workload is, you can figure out the number of hours a person works.

WHY PART-TIME LIES ARE SO COMMON

Lies about passive and part-time income appeal to very human desires. Who doesn't want to get rich without working? If you look at Google search suggestions, you can see that people are constantly looking for "get-rich-quick schemes that work" and "work-from-home jobs."

Recruiters who tell this lie bait prospects with that desire. They want people to believe they've finally stumbled across the one fantastic opportunity that will allow them to work little and still get rich.

Let me be clear. Some people in this industry do indeed get to a point where they work part-time while making a ton of money, but only after they've put in *years of hard work* building up contacts and knowledge.

Recruiters know most people are busy, so they promote the idea that direct marketing can be done in your leisure time and still prove lucrative.

"In no time, you'll have a passive income stream, so you can quit your other job and spend more time with family," they say.

SETTING REALISTIC GOALS

What makes a good income differs from person to person. For some, $100,000 a month is a pay cut; for others, $1,000 a month would be perfectly fine.

Recruiters should ask potential recruits how much money they need to feel happy and successful, then help them match the money they want to the amount of time they're willing to work. If someone wants to make $10,000 a month while working ten minutes a week, they're sure to fail. However, if they're willing to invest twenty to thirty hours a week for twelve months, then getting to $10,000 a month is a realistic goal, especially if they have the support and mentorship they need to avoid rookie mistakes.

Even if the recruit is willing to work twenty hours a week, clarify with them how life might get in the way. What happens if the spouse wants to take a holiday, or one of their kids needs to travel to a tournament. Work with them to come up with two scenarios:

- A perfect-world scenario where everything goes as planned.
- An average scenario that both of you can accept if some things go awry.

The second scenario will help the recruit feel less frustrated if things don't go well. Set an achievable income for the first three-, six-, nine-, and twelve-month milestones to keep the recruit on course and reinforce their commitment.

DOES INFLUENCE PLAY A ROLE?

Influence makes life easier, but most people start their career with none. That makes everything harder in the beginning. When I was a student, I knew nothing about the business world. I studied sports, philosophy, and economics, a mix that made people more suspicious than impressed when I first started pitching products to them. I had absolutely no credibility in the business world, and it made things much harder.

Imagine an internationally known Olympic sprinter going to work for a supplement company. He has an automatic advantage because he has influence with the general public. When he pitches a supplement, people listen because they know he's an expert.

On the other hand, an unknown salesperson who isn't an athlete will have a much harder time. People are attracted to success. When they see successful people pitching a product, they want to know more.

The sprinter is pitching himself as much as he's pitching the product. A professional of any kind, whether an athlete, nutritionist, or telecommunications expert, has status that gives them a boost when making sales. They will always outperform an unknown player with no track record.

The situation is far from hopeless for the unknown recruit, but it's important to clarify where they stand, because they will have to build their career based solely on the product or business.

WHAT SHOULD RECRUITERS SAY INSTEAD?

As always, truth is the best weapon. When you tell the truth, you never need to remember made-up numbers or stories, and you will never be accused of misleading people.

That's the beauty of truth—it makes life easier. Explain

the true income potential of the recruit, given their experience, ambition, influence, and time commitment. Help the recruit develop realistic income goals, based on their desires and potential, and track their progress on a weekly basis.

Tell new recruits that their income will ultimately reflect the time and effort they invest.

You might say, "Before we launch, we're going to look at all factors and determine what kind of outcome you can expect."

That approach builds trust, and if you meet written expectations, you will win the recruit's long-term loyalty.

OTHER LIES ABOUT INVESTMENT

You can't make big money right out of the gate working part-time, and you can't make money without taking a few risks. However, it's so much easier to commit to a company when there's no risk involved, so that's the lie recruiters tell.

LIE
TWELVE

THERE'S NO RISK INVOLVED

Compared to other job opportunities like franchises, the risk in network marketing and MLM is low. The average investment for a new franchise is $350,000. By comparison, a startup package for a network marketing business is rarely more than $100 to $300.

Still, *less risk* isn't the same as *no risk*, and there is more to investment than money.

A GUN TO MY HEAD

As the founder of my own direct marketing company, I have occasionally attracted negative attention. Shortly after the war in Bosnia, I went to meet a banker named Igor Delic in the lobby of the Sheraton Hotel in Zagreb, Croatia. He was the president of Promdej Bank, and I wanted to find out why he wouldn't transfer money to my main bank account. He owed me $7 million USD, but it was parked in the account at his bank, and I wanted to meet with him to make sure he would complete the transfer.

I walked into the hotel and crossed the reception area. It looked like any other five-star hotel. People were enjoying brunch, sipping coffee, and quietly chatting. Igor met me, shook my hand, and invited me to sit at an available table.

As soon as he sat down across from me, he said, "I think you're making too much money."

"What's wrong with making money?" I asked, confused.

"You've got a lot of payments coming into your account," he replied. "I called a few of your customers, and they all seem excited. It makes you seem suspicious."

"Sounds like all my customers are happy," I said. "That's nice feedback. I don't understand what the problem is."

"Well, your customers aren't really the point," Igor said. "The point is, I'm not giving you back your money."

At the time, I'd deposited a total of $6.8 million in the account, so, as you can imagine, I was in full-blown panic mode at the possibility of losing that much money.

Because I was young at the time, I was also a bit crazy, and the anger was building fast. I briefly considered leaping over the table and strangling the guy until he changed his mind.

I stood up, fists clenched.

Suddenly, as if we were in a bad movie, two shady characters in suits came out of nowhere, drew guns, and pressed them to either side of my head. As in *every* bad movie, the guns had these big, ridiculous silencers on them.

"Sit down," Igor said. "I have a proposal for you."

"Okay, fine," I said, sitting slowly. "What is it?"

"My proposal is this: I keep your money, you keep your life."

"That sounds like a fair deal," I said, anger melting immediately into terror. "Can I go home now?"

"Sure," Igor said with a menacing, toothy smile. "Have a safe journey."

I rose again. It felt like a scene in a Western as I turned and walked away. I was sure I would be shot in the back, but I made it out of the hotel, flagged down a cab, and drove straight to the airport.

I hopped a flight back to my company headquarters and tried to figure out how I was going to replace the lost $6.8 million. I contacted my lawyers and asked them to do everything in their power to hunt down Igor Delic and get my money back.

A week later, one of my employees ran into my office and said, "I can't believe you did that!"

"What did I do?" I asked.

"Haven't you seen the news?"

I shook my head.

As it turned out, Igor Delic had been gunned down in front of his bank—shot twenty-six times. It wasn't me. That's not my style. Actually, as it turned out, he had stolen money from both the Mob and the European Union. The EU had chosen his bank to distribute funds for rebuilding Bosnia and parts of Croatia after the war. According to newspapers at the time, he stole between $250 and $500 million from them.

One day, as he was leaving the bank, a car pulled up in front of him, a window rolled down, and gunmen put an end to Igor. I took a small measure of comfort knowing I wasn't the only idiot who had chosen to work with him.

Clearly, he had stolen from the wrong people. I'm just glad I got out of the hotel lobby alive.

There's always a risk.

SOCIAL RISK

Network marketers don't usually run the risk of being shot, but they do risk losing their social network. Once your friends, family, and acquaintances tire of hearing that your product is the best thing since sliced bread, you will start getting fewer invitations to parties. If you push a little too hard, you might end up being labeled "weird."

Over time, unless you make new friends in the network marketing world, you might find that you're all by yourself. That's the social risk you run.

JOB RISK

You also run the risk of losing your primary job. Many companies have contracts that ban unapproved moonlighting, particularly among high-level staff on the career ladder.

People fail to read the fine print of their employment contracts, so they might not even be aware of this restriction.

New recruits need to be aware of this possibility and make sure they know what restrictions their existing companies have placed on them.

LEGAL RISK

Tax agencies are the same in every country. They get mad when you don't pay what you owe. Fortunately, western governments tend to allow many deductions, so if you're not making money yet with your network marketing business, you probably won't pay any taxes.

On the other hand, you have to declare everything properly. If you're not meticulous when you file, you could end up in legal trouble, and companies rarely help their partners with tax procedures. Some companies don't even talk about proper tax filing.

PHYSICAL RISK

Although it only happens at the extreme end of the industry, the kind of risk I encountered in Croatia does occasionally happen. A friend of mine was working for Herbalife in Italy. When I met him for lunch one day, he said, "Have you heard the good news? Colombia is open now. We can build an Herbalife business in Colombia! That's what I'm going to do."

"I don't know if you read the news," I replied, "but there are more shootings in Colombia in a single week than there are in Italy in an entire year. Is that a risk you're willing to take?"

In the end, he opted to continue selling in Italy.

THE PRICE I PAID

I accepted the many risks in this industry, and I occasionally paid the price. When I joined the industry, I lost all my friends, but they didn't leave me. I left them.

I was intensely driven and fully committed to "financing the future" at HMI. I remember in sales pitches, I would say, "I don't mind if you don't buy from me, but I want you to sign a statement that says you understand you will wind up in poverty if you only depend on your savings and pension. You'll be looking for a job at the age of seventy. I want you to sign that statement, so I can rest assured I won't go to hell for contributing to your misery by letting you walk away."

That was my level of commitment in those days. Sadly, I didn't listen to my coaches, who told me, "Don't tell your friends you sell insurance, let alone that you work for an MLM health insurance company. Don't even tell your best friends."

I didn't take their advice, even though they'd been in business for decades. I thought I knew better.

At the time, I used to have a big barbecue in the garden of my home every weekend for my sixteen closest friends. One fateful weekend, I told them.

"Hey, guys, I just started selling insurance with a company called HMI."

They brushed it off. "Sounds crazy, but you're a student anyway. What does it matter?"

"I want to meet with each of you, so I can practice selling," I said. "Skills pay the bills. I won't actually be selling to you, just practicing."

One way or another, every single one of my friends replied, "No thanks. Don't come to my house."

"Hey, guys, aren't we friends?" I asked. "I'm asking you to do this as a friend. I need the help so I can get my business going."

Still, they turned me down.

For years, I had been the most reliable person in my friend group. I was the one who always helped out anyone in need. If a car broke down in the middle of the night, I was the one my friends knew they could call for a ride. Now, at last, it was my turn to ask for a favor, and they all turned me down. None of them would meet with me, even if I was only *practicing* my selling skills.

Finally, angry, I said, "Look, this is the last time I'm talking to any of you. Never come to my house again."

I would perhaps handle it differently now, but at the time, I couldn't believe they wouldn't help me. I made a clean cut and ended my friendships with all of them.

MY LEGAL ADVENTURES

Whenever anyone in this industry experiences success, other people get jealous. At the same time, governments don't like it when a network marketing business gets too big.

I've been careful enough in my career that I've never been sued by either a customer or a business partner. Largely, that's because I've never over-promised or under-delivered. As a company owner, however, I have fought lawsuits in eleven different countries, trying to fend off established companies that didn't want a new competitor moving into their market.

Many of those established companies have relationships

with their respective governments, so a few whispered accusations can cause real problems.

"Hey, we think this new guy might be selling secondhand products as new products, and we've heard they're not paying international taxes."

That sort of gossip-mongering led to a number of government lawsuits and a lot of headaches. Fortunately, I have won every single court case against me and my companies. Still, the amount of time, money, and effort spent fighting them was exhausting.

LEGAL ISSUES AT EACH STAGE OF YOUR CAREER

Your legal risks vary depending on where you are on the career ladder. Marketing companies love to tell new recruits that they can't be sued, and in most countries, this is true. However, the situation can change in a moment if a government body like the FTC declares your company a scam.

The moment that happens, all your company protection is gone, and anyone who signed up for the company, even as a customer, will likely be investigated. Individual responsibility will be based on the amount of money that's missing (if any) and the structure of the business.

Even people with a lifetime income of $50,000 can be targeted to recover missing money.

This scenario has played out many times in recent years. So many people thought cryptocurrency companies would be a safe, no-risk investment, but they're now getting hammered by lawsuits. One of the biggest financial authorities in Europe, Germany's BaFin, decided that cryptocurrency is technically an investment, so now every single distributor of cryptocurrency must have government approval. This decision opens the door to lawsuits against any and every distributor in an organization.

HIDDEN EXPENDITURES

Companies love to say the starter pack is the only money new recruits have to spend, but this is far from the truth. There are many other expenses to starting and growing a marketing business. First, you have to attend big regional events, as well as regular meetings. Some of these cost money, and while the fees might be small, they add up.

When you start attending the big conventions, you will have travel expenses like hotels and airfare. Many of the destinations for these conventions aren't cheap either. In most big cities around the world, you can easily spend $300 a night on a hotel room.

When you're selling, you have to meet people somewhere. People often use reception areas of hotels, but Starbucks is also popular. Expect to buy both yourself and your prospect drinks. It looks fishy to ask your prospect to pay for their own coffee. "Why are you so cheap, if you're making big money?" Still, these coffees add up. Buying a three-dollar coffee for two people eight times a day for five days in a row costs you $240 a week.

There are other unexpected costs. You might be pushed to buy more inventory at the end of the month to help the team hit a goal. The team leader might say, "I'm trying to get us to the next rank. If you pitch in now, I will help you later."

You might also have to pay for personal development events that your company believes are necessary. While personal development certainly helps, it's not cheap. A top coach can charge anywhere from $300 to $2,000. Ideally, a company should warn new recruits that there's a huge personal development cost, so everyone is on the same page.

In light of these expenses, claiming there's *no risk* becomes an obvious lie.

THE TRUTH ABOUT RISK

Life's lack of safety is my personal guarantee. You might not have guns pressed to your head, but with any new endeavor in which you can make big money, challenges are inevitable.

From taxes and unexpected expenses to lawsuits and lost friends, a lot can (and will) happen to you. Even if you get to the point where you're making $100,000 a month, life won't always be easy. That kind of money opens up many opportunities, but it also stirs up trouble.

One of the biggest challenges is fending off the sharks who begin to circle, and the biggest sharks in the ocean are investment bankers. They smell that growing pile of money from a mile away, and they would love to get a piece of it. Be very wary of their investment schemes.

Taxes can also take you by surprise. If you make $800,000 in a year but fail to set aside enough money to pay your massive tax bill, you might wind up in jail.

Every level of your career will present you with particular challenges. As a friend of mine likes to say, "New levels, new devils." There is no straight line to the top. It's a roller coaster all the way. Just about the time you think everything is going well, another obstacle appears in the distance. All you can do is get past it and win another deal. These are the risks you run. It's part of the deal.

To protect yourself, invest a portion of your money so you can handle the unexpected. When problems arise, don't give up, particularly in the first year. If you can't commit twelve months to this business, don't bother signing up.

Even the greatest product on the market needs twelve months. I have never seen big success happen faster than that.

In his book *Outliers*, Malcolm Gladwell argues that mastering any skill requires 20,000 hours. Divide that by five years and you'll see how many hours you need to commit each month for the first year to succeed. (That comes to almost eleven hours a day over those 1,825 days.)

Too often, recruits are given promises about what they can achieve, but they aren't given the "how." You have to understand how much time and hard work it's going to take to master your business.

Potential new recruits deserve to know that there are risks in this industry. The biggest risk is that you will invest a lot of time, money, and effort and not experience real success for the first year. Remember, I'd made a grand total of less than $500 by the end of my eleventh month.

Are you willing to keep plugging away until the big checks start rolling in? Are you willing to keep plugging away even if you lose your fake friends and destroy your social life for a little while? Real friends will stick with you anyway, and they will appreciate your drive to succeed. If so, you can achieve the big success you've always dreamed of. The money is there if you want it.

CONCLUSION

Network marketing could be such a wonderful industry. When I think about that, I get angry. When I observe all of the lies and manipulation that sully the reputation of this industry, I get furious. There's no reason for it. The truth is powerful enough, and, more than that, potential new recruits *deserve* the truth.

So, here's the truth.

If you don't take ownership of your success and apply the lessons in this book, you will have a bad experience with network marketing. Like millions of others, you will work hard and still wind up worse off than when you began.

Great opportunities exist. No other industry creates more income, and all the hard work is worth it, but you have to enter this industry wisely.

HOW TO AVOID BEING TAKEN FOR A RIDE

First, decide what kind of company is a good fit for you. Think about the kind of leadership and company culture you need. There are plenty of fantastic products out there, but not all of them are sold by companies that align with your needs. You might not agree with their marketing strategy, sales process, or even their verbiage. Think about who you are and who you want to represent.

This industry thrives off synergy. Companies need you in order to profit, and you need them in order to grow and change your life for the better. Therefore, it's important to know with whom you are working.

Let the lessons of this book help you choose wisely. You now have a checklist for weeding out the bad actors.

Next, determine your level of involvement. Take care not to set yourself up for failure by selecting an impossible goal. If you set a goal to make $100,000 a month, you are committing yourself to a lot of work. It must be clear to you, your spouse, and everyone who shares your life just how much time you'll be spending on the business.

Finally, you should commit to working for twelve months to give it a fair shot. If you can't commit to twelve months, don't bother signing up. This industry is not for you. As a matter of fact, being self-employed might not be right for you.

There are no guarantees in life. Even with this book as a guide, you might pick the wrong company. I have worked, both directly and indirectly, as a consultant for seventy-six different companies in various verticals and markets, all related to direct marketing. Along the way, I've invested money with some of them only to watch the company shut down and disappear. In a couple of cases, the founders decided they'd made enough money and shuttered their companies. While it's technically illegal to shut a company down like that, it still happened, and I lost out.

Though it's impossible to predict the future with 100 percent success, by applying the tips in this book, you will avoid a lot of pain.

For industry leaders and recruiters who read this book, I challenge you to embrace a better way. Though exposing common lies might sound like I'm pointing accusatory fingers, the truth is, when you point your finger at someone else, you point three fingers right back at yourself. I've had to embrace a better and more honest way myself.

If you use the honest methods described in this book, people will stay longer and be more satisfied with the work. They will work more efficiently, and your company will enjoy greater success. Working together, we will also begin to change the reputation of your companies and our industry.

In the end, everyone wins.

ABOUT THE AUTHOR

MARK DAVENPORT is the professional and pen name of a well-known serial entrepreneur and marketing expert who has started more than nineteen companies in fields as diverse as direct marketing, software, nano-technology, and automated marketing. Having sold all of his ventures, the author now lives in Dubai, where he continues to advise entrepreneurs and direct marketing companies around the world.

9 781544 503943